Precision Prospect Development

By

Nathan Isaiah Fay

A Precision Philanthropy Publication

ISBN-13: 978-0-578-44419-2

DEDICATION

Lokah Samastah Sukhino Bhavantu.

May all beings everywhere be happy and free, and may the thoughts, words, and actions of my life contribute to that happiness and freedom.

CONTENTS

PREFACE

"To live life most fully, one had to risk suffering and overcome it."

Nietzsche

Poverty, disease, starvation, human trafficking, earthquakes, floods, hurricanes, homelessness, racism, violence and war are just a few of the problems that are currently wreaking havoc on our planet, our lives, and affecting the welfare of all living beings who call this earth home. The non-profit sector is the only sector that is 100%-dedicated to combating these ills of earth so that as many living beings as possible can live a life of unbounded self-expression, freedom and creativity in peace and harmony with the Earth and with each other. Unfortunately for the world, however noble our collective intentions may be, the non-profit sector is not operating at its highest potential. The non-profit industry is stuck in a rut. It is operating at half-mast. It is in need of a serious overhaul if it is going to reach its fullest potential.

The non-profit sector is at a critical inflection point. If non-profits continue to operate with little to no investment or interest in their data infrastructures, then the industry as we know it could cease to exist and the problems of the world will only continue to get worse. A new era of philanthropy is needed. The elements required to usher in this new era of philanthropy are no longer off in the distant horizon[1]. They are here now.

However, in order for this new era to happen, Prospect Development departments must step up their collective game and lead the way.

Prospect Development is currently vastly underrepresented at the senior leadership table. In order to get our seat and help to steer our organizations on course for success, some key changes need to take place. It will require a new mindset. It will require a new way of conducting business. It will require the implementation of *Precision Prospect Development.* This book is dedicated to inspiring you equipping you with the toolkit to take your department to the next level and to finally get a seat at the leadership table so that you can have maximum impact.

The world needs us to step up and speak out. The world needs us to thrive. The world needs us to expand our reach. The world needs us to operate at our highest potential so that we can eliminate all of the negativities that are preventing the world and all of the living beings within it from operating at their highest potential. If we can achieve this, we will bring far more credence to our oft-stated ethos and desire to make the world a better place.

---

[1] The new era is ***Precision Philanthropy***. See, Precision Philanthropy Artificial Intelligence and the Future of Generosity for more on the new era of philanthropy.

Chapter 1

PRECISION PROSPECT DEVELOPMENT

"It is the mark of an educated person to look for precision in each class of things just so far as the nature of the subject admits."

Aristotle

Each non-profit organization is a living entity made up of a multitude of moving parts; employees, donors, volunteers, finances, technology, departments, world events, leadership, goals, mission, and more. All of these elements combined together create the collective ecosystem within which each shop operates. What works at one organization will not necessarily work at another, might need to be modified, or might work at another organization a year from now. Because we operate in this living, cybernetic collective environment, one size does not fit all when it comes to developing your Prospect Development program and implementing strategies. We must therefore pay primary attention to all of the unique elements that make up our collective and align our activities in a way that speaks to the uniqueness of our organization and the uniqueness of each moment of time within our organization as well. The advice in this book is flexible so that you can custom tune it and apply it to your individual circumstances.

Precision Prospect Development utilizes the *six elements of precision*[2] to plug into the unique DNA of an organization in order to sync all activities so as to operate in a seamless fashion that will best meet the needs of the organization, further the mission, and optimize the donor experience. *Precision Prospect Development* is all about maximizing impact through custom-tailoring business processes: right time, right place, right people, right project, right delivery method, right prospect, right ask. All activities must be connected to the collective in a way that will allow for impact.

Precision Prospect Development is also all about laying the foundations to implement *the platform* that will make *Precision Philanthropy*[3] possible, as well as building out the systems necessary to allow your organization to relate to each constituent in a customizable and unique way based on their current position and passions.

Precision Prospect Development is all about the distillation of data into actionable intelligence that is precisely pinpointed to match each and every prospect with a *programmatic pathway*. A ***programmatic pathway*** is a tailored approach that addresses the uniqueness of each individual or group in the constituent base and shapes the approach to match the uniqueness of any given environment and for any given desired outcome.

Through the creation, adoption and implementation of *Precision Prospect Development* departments across all non-profits, we will usher in the era of *Precision Philanthropy*. We will optimize the donor experience in a way that was previously impossible and will therefore push forward all non-profit missions further than ever thought possible. We will ensure healthy growth in philanthropic revenue across all organizations, thus increasing the overall benefit for humanity. We will make sure that every organization that has a VP of Fundraising will also have a VP of Prospect Development. If we can accomplish this, the impact on the planet will be exponential.

---

[2] See chapter, "The Six Key Elements for Precision."

[3] *Precision Philanthropy* is a term coined by Nathan Fay to describe a future-state, cybernetic structure, that utilizes artificial intelligence technologies to dramatically enhance efficiency in the nonprofit sector. Precision Philanthropy utilizes artificial intelligence technologies to unlock generosity and align individuals with non-profit missions at the intersection of passion and purpose.

Chapter 2

WHO IS THIS BOOK FOR?

This book is a must read for anyone working in the non-profit sector.

If you are a ***non-profit executive***, you cannot effectively run your organization without understanding the deep and reaching impact of data. You must ensure the creation of a world-class data infrastructure to support your program. This book will help you understand how valuable a highly functioning P*recision Prospect Development* department is to your bottom line and the success of your organization.

If you are on the front lines as a ***fundraiser*** and want to know how to best partner with Prospect Development to ensure that you are focusing on the right information and getting best in class service, data, reports, and prospects, then this book is for you. You will also learn some great ways to increase your revenue and get the most out of your data so that you raise more money than ever.

If you work under the ***Prospect Development, Advancement Services, Business Intelligence, Data Science and Data Analytics*** umbrella in the non-profit space, you will benefit greatly from this book. It is meant for both beginner and master. This is for us data folks to help elevate our field and ensure our work will have the greatest impact.

The interconnectedness of the work that is done by all of these teams demands that each member has a deep understanding of the roles and responsibilities of each department. Our current environment demands deep cross-operational knowledge and understanding. The strategies deployed by any one given unit under the Prospect Development or Advancement Services umbrella must be aligned with leadership and the higher strategies of actionable intelligence, data distillation, value proposition, identifying the best prospects and matching them with the right fundraisers, thereby increasing efficiency, increasing fundraising revenue and building *the platform*.

Chapter 3

WHY PRECISION PROSPECT DEVELOPMENT

Precision Prospect Development *utilizes precision to build and maintain a connected, living, sustainable, cybernetic structure through which we collect, analyze and distill data into actionable intelligence to increase efficiency, solve business challenges, drive strategy and increase revenue.*

We are drowning in data. There is more data available to us now than there has ever been and the amount of data that we are faced with is only going to increase. A non-profit organization is made up of various fundraising units, and each one has its own portfolio of engagement and giving opportunities available to its constituents. We can think of these opportunities as pathways that lead to the fulfillment of an organization's mission. The goal is to pinpoint as many constituents as possible and match them with a *programmatic pathway* that they are passionate about, which will maximize partnership, engagement, and giving ultimately leading to the fulfillment the organization's mission.

The mission of Prospect Development is to properly capture and manage an organization's data, constantly turning it into *actionable intelligence* that matches as many constituents as possible with each department's pathways. Combined with algorithmic guidance on how to best ensure as many successful journeys down the various pathways occur, this can optimize the donor experience while maximizing revenue and efficiency.

In order to achieve this, we must have a seat at the table. We must have influence in our organizations, great relationships with our stakeholders, and master the art of distillation. We must think like a fundraiser, mastering the fundamentals and focusing on the bottom line. We must plug into our organization's DNA, and develop a platform that allows for precision prospect matching.

With increased awareness of the value and the pivotal role that data plays in philanthropy, more and more organizations across the globe are investing in their dataverses to increase organizational effectiveness and to bring more dollars in the door. In order to manage this endeavor, there is a rising need for someone at the table who understands the organization's data and can translate that into actionable intelligence that is easily digestible to senior leadership and development professionals. This is no small feat and when done properly is a highly valuable one. Historically underrepresented at the AVP and VP level, Prospect Development is currently being invited more and more to the table at various organizations. However, this is not happening nearly enough, nor is it happening at a fast enough rate.

If you employ the strategies and tactics contained in this book, and practice *Precision Prospect Development*, you will be able to ride the wave of big data into the executive office as an influencer. Your rate of successful project implementation, relationships with your colleagues, and efficiency will improve. You will receive more resources, your impact will increase exponentially, and your organization will raise more money. You'll enjoy your work more, spin your wheels less, and be more connected to your stakeholders and to your organization's mission.

Most importantly, you'll optimize the donor experience, maximize revenue and efficiency, help your organization fulfill its mission and help to make the world a better place while setting up the appropriate infrastructure to carry all of this out. It is becoming increasingly obvious that non-profits must not only embrace data, but also employ skilled data workers to create systems and effectively deploy them throughout the office. This will not be cheap. Pay and status must be in alignment with the required skills and job function in order to attract top talent that can make this possibility a reality.

Now is the time. We must strike while the iron is hot. Never has there been a more suitable environment for leadership to see the value of data and those who work with it. Immerse yourself in the following pages and get your seat at the table.

I have been practicing and perfecting the tactics outlined in this book my entire life, studying the fundamentals of this approach since I was a child; after earning my bachelor and master degree, I began my career in development back in 2005, and in just over ten years, through the utilization of these tactics, I was able to achieve considerable success in our field. I started out as a gift processor at Stanford and quickly moved to assistant director, then to director, and have been associate vice president for a few years. I am currently one of only a handful of folks in our field who has managed to make it to the senior leadership level. Having experienced what can be accomplished when actually given the opportunity to provide leadership to an organization at a high level from the data perspective I am even more shocked that this is not the norm for every organization. I understand the struggle and frustrations that come along with not having a voice or being able to drive strategy or operate your program in the way that can best benefit your organization due to limited power emanating from placement in a lower level of the organizational hierarchy. In hopes that more and more of us can achieve this stature in our organizations, I have outlined a strategy in this book that helped me to push the boundaries, break down the walls and barriers and rise up to ensure that our organizations are able to take full advantage of the value that our field has to offer. This is a long-standing issue and one that we are finally going to overcome together. We cannot give up. In the words of Woody Guthrie, "This land was made for you and me."

Chapter 4

Tactical *(The What)* + Philosophical *(The How)*

"Every person must decide whether they will walk in the light of creative altruism or in the darkness of destructive selfishness."

Martin Luther King, Jr.

Google performed a study in 2013 on large amounts of its employee data called *Project Oxygen*. They analyzed all of their hiring and performance data, looking to hone in on the characteristics that made for the best employees. To Google's surprise, technical skills (or STEM skills) were the least-important indicators of success, whereas all of the top characteristics that determined success were all soft skills, like being a good listener, or having compassion and empathy.

This book is broken into two different types of advice: *The What* (tactical), and *The* How (philosophical soft skills*)*. The Google study mentioned above mirrors my own experience. What I learned growing up and in the workforce is that focusing on tactical skills alone is never enough to ensure success. In fact, being a strict master of the tactical alone can actually hinder your advancement and your influence within an organization if it is not appropriately balanced with a mastery of *The How*. Many data folks are under the false impression that through simply mastering tactical/technical skills that they will achieve success, garner influence and get a seat at the table. But this is not true. Tactical advice can only take you so far. Implementation of tactical advice alone will rarely lead to success. Life does not operate that way. There are too many other variables at play. This is where *The How* comes into play. How you deliver content is far more important than the content you deliver. How you deliver content changes the meaning of the content delivered.[4]

This book pairs tactical advice and strategies with a heavy emphasis on practical and philosophical ways of approaching your work life that will ensure the successful implementation of projects, positive impact, increasing the bottom line, increasing efficiencies, and an increase in influence culminating in a seat at the table.

[4] See chapter "How vs. What" for more on the interplay of these two variables

Chapter 5

IT'S ALL ABOUT THE DATA

Warning, data paradigm shift ahead.

We are champions of data. We are masters of analytics. We eat, breathe, and sleep information for a living. As data professionals, we are all about the data at all times, but not in every way.

Not in every way? How is this possible?

We actually overlook a majority of the data that is vital for our work to succeed. What data is that? It is the data that is all around us, in other words, the data of our current collective state. The data around us is made up of the data of our organization's DNA, the data that makes up *The Who, What, When, Where, Why*, and *How* (the *six elements)* of the present moment.[5]

[5] See chapter, "The Six Key Elements for Precision," for more on the importance of the *Who, What, When, Where, Why* and *How*

We have institutional and demographic data for days on prospects and donors. We have predictive modeling that can tell us how much a certain donor might give, or how likely they are to make a certain kind of donation. We have data that tracks the interactions of fundraisers with donors. We have advanced methods for understanding this data and extracting value from it. When most of us think about data, we think about the data sets that reside in our databases on our donors and on the activity of our fundraisers because we are so deeply entrenched in figuring out how to generate actionable intelligence for our constituents.

Most of us don't realize that this is only a part of the equation; this might not even be the most important part of the equation for success. The data that we need to become better at understanding, processing and predicting is the collective data of our organization's DNA. The data of our fundraisers, our office settings, our technology infrastructures, our departments. The data that makes up *The Who, What, When, Where, Why*, and *How* of all of the activities, strategies and personalities floating around our office. Master this dataset and the world is your oyster. Incorporate this data into how you operate, and allow this data to inform you on each and everything that you do. Utilize your highly advanced, fine-tuned analytical skills on this dataset to inform your operations.

There is subtlety in the message of this book. The advice is "alive," so to speak. Don't fall into the pit of "We tried this before and it didn't work." That way of thinking and approaching your work or life will not serve you well. That way of thinking removes your power to be a change agent and equates to making an excuse and thus falling victim to excusitis. The times are different now. Sometimes it takes a few attempts to have a new approach take hold. You might not have had the right people in the room or taken the right approach. It may be so simple that a past project failed because your manager or your constituents were having a bad day. It's nearly impossible to do the same thing twice because of all of the differing variables at play combined with the fact that the essence of life is change.

We live in the physical world with time and space. Re-creating all of the same variables from one time to another is not possible. This reminds me of the movie Jurassic Park. If the dinosaurs in the original Jurassic Park didn't continue to check the electric fences for weaknesses they would not have been able to break free from their captivity once the electricity was shut down. Had they resigned themselves to their circumstances, they would have missed their window of opportunity to make a change. Stay alert and be ready to move when the data of the six elements indicates that a particular *next best action*[6] is recommended. This will be the way that you can successfully implement ideas even if they have been rejected multiple times by the same person. You have the power to change your circumstances in any and every situation you face. Never forget this.

If you want your work to have impact, if you want your seat at the table, if you want your organization to thrive, you must allow this data to drive the *six elements* of everything you do.

Welcome to the world of precision living. Welcome to the world of *Precision Prospect Development.* What are you going to do with this knowledge? What are you going to do when you have mastered your full dataset? When you focus on this additional dataset, you can build your own internal algorithms that will allow you to gain the ability to overcome any and every obstacle you face. There will only be abundance. There will only be yes. There will only be success. What kind of a difference are you going to make?

[6] See Chapter 37 "Next Best Action" for more on this concept.

Chapter 6

What Kind of Difference Are You Going to Make?

"You cannot get through a single day without having an impact on the world around you. What you do makes a difference. And you have to decide what kind of difference you want to make."

Jane Goodall

As children, we exhibit a never-ending curiosity about the world around us. The question "why?" is always on our lips. We operate as little sponges, constantly absorbing as much data about the world around us as possible, connecting dots, increasing our awareness and attempting to understand the nature of life and the rules that govern it. As we move into adulthood, the frequency with which we question the world around us, including the assumptions and general knowledge of others, decreases exponentially.

Why is this the case? By the time we reach adulthood, we have generally collected enough data to feel fairly confident that we have enough of a grasp of the world around us to move through life successfully. Along with this confidence in our foundational knowledge of the world, we also tend to have a greater tendency to accept things as they are presented to us as facts of life if they are in no obvious conflict with our foundational structure of awareness. We tend to accept more and more that reality is how it is presented to us and factualize possibilities. Things are the way they are because that's life and that's the way things are; accept and move on.

Many influencers understand that the opposite is true and do not settle for this worldview. They don't ever stop asking why. They don't stop challenging their assumptions or the assumptions of others. They dig deeper into cause and effect. The world is malleable. The world is ours. The structures of the world that we were thrown into at birth were created by the previous generations, people who were no smarter and no different than us. Steve Jobs calls this realization a "profound truth" that once realized will alter the course of your life forever.[7]

Once this truth is realized, you will interact with the world in a much different way. You will understand the impact that your presence can have at a deeper level. Your creations can change the world; your actions can alter the course of history. Broaden your horizons of what you are capable of accomplishing and don't impose limitations on yourself. Don't allow fear to stop you from expressing your genius, from speaking out and speaking up.

Don't settle for the status quo in your office, subscribing to bad habits and bad processes because "that's the way things have always been done." Don't settle for small, or, shortsighted thinking. Constantly look at the world and your work with a fresh pair of eyes.

---

[7] Silicon Valley Historical Association Interview with Steve Jobs at NeXT Computer, Redwood City, 1995

Know that what came before you was created at a different time to meet the unique needs of the time. In addition, what came before you was created by others with their own set of limitations. As you work on every project, examine it and look for patterns as well as potential efficiencies.

Don't be afraid to make adjustments. Don't be afraid to stop doing certain things altogether if they are no longer relevant or if the ROI no longer justifies the effort. Never stop questioning. Never stop asking why. *The Why* is one of the most powerful tools you have in your *Precision Prospect Development* toolbox.

I suggest doing this exercise when working through a project. Ask the following set of questions guided by the *six elements* of precision:

- *Who* is this for? *Who* does this affect?
- *What* is the desired outcome? *What* is this for?
- *When* is the optimal time to begin and end?
- *Where* will it take place?
- *Why* are we doing this?
- *How* should we implement?

By answering these questions, you can refine the process of solutioning and hone in on the best possible solution that meets the goal of the project and has the greatest impact. This will allow you to the peel away any unnecessary layers and only do the work that is necessary for optimal results.

Think about what difference you want to make in your organization and with your life in general. Take the steps necessary to implement that difference. You can't avoid making a difference. Let's say you are unhappy with your current office culture or structure and decide to just phone it in and not even try to improve your conditions. Through inaction, you are influencing the culture to remain the same and to possibly get worse for you. Don't phone it in. Never settle. Remain as conscious as possible of your impact. Keep your light on and let it shine.

Examine your current state of being and how you interact with the world; understand your current trajectory and current impact and ask yourself, "Is this the impact I want to make? Is this in alignment with my goals? Is this going to help my organization optimize the donor experience and help fulfill our mission?"

Experiment with your life and your actions. Adopt a playful attitude and try different strategies to implement change. Observe the results, refine your approach and try again. Continue to craft your personal key to unlock the changes that only you can make. We can all be master keymakers with the ability to unlock the door to the source of anything.

Let's not settle for the status quo in our organizations and let's not be afraid to shake things up a bit and turn things on their heads. Let's get senior leadership to think of Prospect Development folks as revenue generators, as fundraisers; let's get our seat at the table and exert our influence for the greater good of our donors, our mission, our organization, our profession and our world.

Chapter 7

GETTING A SEAT AT THE TABLE

"It tastes better when you share."

Unknown Prussian Proverb

We all want a seat at the table, but we all don't have one. I want all of us to have one. This entire book is directed to the advancement of our field on all levels and this includes the advancement of our place within the hierarchical structure of the development office. As stated in the opening chapter, "Why *Precision Prospect Development*," this entire book is based on strategies I implemented in my own career that resulted in getting a seat at the table in every role I held. In order for our organizations to take full advantage of their data and to achieve the highest ROI, Prospect Development must be invited to the senior leadership table and given a permanent seat.

In order for Prospect Development to get an invite to the senior leadership table, we must make some key changes to the way in which we see ourselves, the way in which we present ourselves, the way in which we conduct our business, and how we operate as a whole. We must do our part to get invited. If you are not currently at the table, there is likely a reason. We must own this, even if the lack of representation doesn't appear to be due to any fault of our own. This might be a hard truth to accept. Take a look at your program and the activities that you are allocating your resources to. Make sure that they are in alignment with your organization's mission and goals, and that they are promoting the donor experience and driving revenue. Make sure that you are speaking the right language at work to position your program in the best possible light.

One common answer that we give ourselves is that our lack of representation is because the fundraisers or senior leadership just don't get us or understand our value, and that no matter what we do they will never understand. When we buy into this paradigm, we are removing our power to influence and settling for a negative, static worldview that does not serve us or our profession. You will find many enablers at our annual conference who are imprisoned by this belief; try your best to not give into this worldview as it is an easy one to buy into. This worldview doesn't just take away your power but it also takes away your responsibility for co-creating this dynamic. Once you have solidified this belief, you are doomed and will live a *Groundhog Day*- like existence and will have a hard time having the impact and influence that you could achieve or should achieve.

The only way to break free and change this negative dynamic into a positive one is to first take full ownership our role in creating and/or sustaining this dynamic. If the dynamic exists and you are a part of it you do have the ability to incite change. It will require stretching yourself and learning new tactics and tools to initiate a momentum to push the pendulum into a more positive, collaborative structure. You do have the power to course correct and create the environment in your office that you have always dreamed of. Think big.

At the time of the writing of this chapter, if you ran some basic searches on LinkedIn or Google, you will find that there are only a handful of folks at the AVP or VP level in our field. If you run the same search for every other department in a development shop, be it annual giving, planned giving, major giving, corporate giving, foundation giving, principal giving, you will find that the complete opposite is true. For practically every organization that has a mature or large development shop with at least 30 employees, there will exist an AVP and/or VP in each of these areas. Notice the pattern here? All of these departments have the word "giving" at the end. We will speak to this later in the book[8], but I just wanted to draw your attention to that here.

This doesn't sit well with me. This has to change. Why are we so underrepresented at the table? Why do we need to have the occasional champion on the front-lines write articles on their blog or on LinkedIn, cheerleading our value proposition to their peers as if our value proposition needs defending, as if it is not widely accepted amongst all organizations that Prospect Development is an essential piece of the development puzzle, and that to muzzle us by not giving us a seat at the table is detrimental to an organization's health? An understanding of *The Why* can help us to quickly correct this travesty so that future generations of Prospect Development folks will be amazed to learn that their pioneering predecessors ever had anything but the seat of honor at the leadership table.

We need to change our categorization in the hierarchy of development from cost center to revenue generator. Follow the advice set in this book and I can guarantee that not only will your department get a seat at the senior leadership table but you will be invited to it. ***Now is our time.*** There has never been any other time in the history of Prospect Development in which our value is so apparent.

---

[8] See Chapter 20 "Prospect Development as a Revenue Generator" and Chapter 21 "Our Value Proposition" for a deeper dive into this topic and for actionable solutions to dramatically swing the pendulum in your favor.

The wave of big data and artificial intelligence technology is here and the surf is amazing. Grab your boards and let's ride the wave to our seat at the table together. Life is too short.

Let's think big together. Ten years from now (or less) the landscape will be vastly different. Any non-profit that has an AVP or VP of Major/Principal Gifts will also have an AVP/VP of Prospect Development and/or a Chief Digital Officer/Chief Data Officer. But we must act now in order for that vision of the future to come to fruition. Senior leadership is becoming more and more aware of the gaps in their data infrastructures and will soon need to find someone to fill them. Will it be you? I certainly hope so.

If you already have a seat at the table, that is awesome news! You are ahead of the curve. You will be able to run faster with the advice outlined in this book and move faster to the creation of the platform that will optimize donor experience and further your organization's mission.

As we push along on this journey, the words of ***the little engine that could*** resonate and reverberate:

I think I can. I think I can. I think I can.

I think I can. I think I can. I think I can.

I --- think --- I --- can --- I --- think --- I --- can --- I --- think -- I - can

Chapter 8

ABUNDANCE CONSCIOUSNESS VS. LACK CONSCIOUSNESS

"Emancipate yourselves from mental slavery, none but ourselves can free our minds."

Bob Marley

One of the mindsets that I've encountered all too often while working in this field and attending conferences on Prospect Development, Data Analytics and Advancement Services over the past ten years has been that of lack consciousness. Whether it be the lack of a seat at the table, the lack of self-belief, the lack of a feeling of influence, the lack of buy-in from senior leadership, the lack of relationships with fundraisers, the lack of respect, lack of resources, lack of praise. The theme is the same: lack. For many years, I was an active participant in such discussions and had allowed this lack consciousness to take root in my mind and to drive my experience.

It wasn't until I addressed this within myself and adopted the strategies outlined in this book that my experiences began to change, as well.

When I began working in Prospect Development, I didn't feel valued by the constituents I supported. I didn't think that my contributions were understood or recognized. Often, I felt like I was delivering gold only to have the recipient toss it away with the rest of the trash. Meetings would take place in which I knew I would add value, but since I was not on the organizers' radar, I was not invited. I joined my fellow colleagues in conversations of frustration and we bonded in our shared experiences. It felt like no matter what I did, there would always be a high percentage of my work that either fell on deaf ears, did not spark action, or was simply ignored. It seemed like this dynamic was imbedded so deeply in the structure of my office that it couldn't be changed.

I wanted to have an impact. I wanted to be an influencer. I wanted to be on the top of the minds of the fundraisers I supported when they were faced with a prospect or data challenge. I wanted to be a true partner with senior leadership and offer my insight at strategy sessions. I wanted to be someone senior leadership would turn to when they had a big challenge that required advanced analytical skills.

One day, out of frustration, I decided to no longer accept this as my fate. I could not go on any longer in a role that was undervalued, watching my work be ignored or misunderstood, working against the current of my constituents and organization. I understood the importance and value of the work that I was doing. I felt both responsible as well as compelled to try to change this dynamic. I knew intuitively and practically that change had to occur if our organizations were going to continue to be successful. I took a step back and began to examine our department's internal dynamics as well as our position in the hierarchical structure of the office. I looked at my role in perpetuating this dynamic and sought areas of improvement and looked for things that I could change.

Some of the questions I asked myself were: What am I responsible for? How am I participating in the current office dynamics? How am I perceived by my colleagues? Why isn't my director a part of the senior leadership team? How is my department viewed by the rest of the organization? What is the actual value we bring to the table? What is the perception of our value by our colleagues? How can I make sure that my work is valued? How do I position myself so that my actionable intelligence inspires action? How do I build better relationships with my constituents? How do I make sure that I come to mind when fundraisers schedule strategy meetings? What am I doing to elevate my department within the office culture? What changes can I make to myself to advance our work?

One of the first things that I realized was that ***this lack consciousness I was carrying around wasn't just a reaction to my current situation, but that it was also a key driver in perpetuating this negative dynamic*** between myself and my constituents. One of the main reasons why we are not positioned in the proper hierarchical structure in our offices that mirrors our worth has a lot to do with lack consciousness. It has always puzzled me as to how it came to be that we have not always held a seat at the table, given the prime real estate that we occupy in the organizational structure that touches all departments and feeds a holistic picture of the office to us on a daily basis.

Carrying around lack consciousness is like carrying around a double-edged sword. For those who are stuck in this mindset, it permeates their entire being and gives off this vibe of weakness. It begins to create the very experiences that perpetuate its existence. It is palpable and will definitely have an impact on your ability to influence and achieve success. You'll be seen like an *Eeyore* figure in the office, always anticipating failure and accepting it. Actually you'll be creating it unwittingly through carrying this negative energy and negative belief system around with you.

Prospect Development is at the center of the wheel of philanthropy. It is in an enviable position in which connection and influence should come naturally, but more often than not that doesn't seem to be happening for many in the field. Why is this the case? Take a step back from yourself and observe your behavior. Observe your beliefs about yourself and about your work. Observe how you are interacting with colleagues, how you come across, what energy you are actually giving off versus what you think you are giving off.

Beliefs and attitudes drive experience and determine destinations. One of the first things that you can do to improve your situation is to remove any lack consciousness from your mind. Don't allow negativity to take control. If you approach your work or your colleagues with an aura of lack, you are doomed from the start. Your presence will not instill confidence. Change your attitude from negative to positive, fill that glass full, and see things from an abundant state. Reinterpret your experience through the lens of positivity.

Adopt a positive mindset no matter what you are faced with. If something doesn't work out in the short term, stay positive and keep at it and understand that it just might be something that needs more time to change, or your approach needs a slight recalibration. I guarantee that if you keep positive, whatever the situation is, or how hopeless it may seem, it will eventually change.

Think big. Remove small thinking from your mind. Remove your focus from limitations. Give yourself the permission to think big and to dream big. All major accomplishments throughout history were first conceived as big ideas. Big ideas move mountains. If those that conceived of them gave up when someone said 'that's not possible', or, 'we tried that before and it didn't work', the world would look vastly different and we'd be a few thousand years behind with our advancements and achievements in all disciplines. Let's think and dream big with what we want to accomplish as individuals and collectively as data professionals. ***Don't confuse a mind block with a road block.*** When someone approaches you with the phrase, 'we tried this before and it didn't work.' Take that as a challenge and let it fuel your efforts to actualize it into being.

We couldn't be in a better place. ***Success is inevitable.*** Large gifts are inevitable. Don't get caught up in the weeds and let small things irritate you. Don't let a few fundraiser data mistakes or misunderstandings throw you off course. Don't get confused as to what a real loss is, as opposed to what is just business as usual. Keep your head up and remain confident that in the long run success is inevitable. Your work will not be in vain.

If you implement the strategies in this book, I guarantee you abundance. You will gain more influence. You will be given more resources. You will have the fundraisers at your fingertips, dying to take you out to lunch. You will be an influencer, with your opinion and presence in high demand. You will not have to ask for your seat at the table, or break into the board room and take one by force. Rather, you will be invited to the table and your presence will be indispensable. You deserve this. Your organization deserves this. Those that your non-profit serve deserve that additional revenue that you will generate through having a greater influence on the bottom line. Your donors deserve the better experience they will have when your work has maximum impact.

Chapter 9

ACTIONABLE INTELLIGENCE

"Is this actionable? Is this going to prompt some sort of action by the recipient or get them closer to taking the *next best action* at the right time?"

Actionable Intelligence Litmus Test

Actionable Intelligence refers to any data that prompts action by the recipient of that data or pushes the recipient closer to the tipping point of action. For example, a researcher just read in the paper that a top donor joined a local board. By pushing this information out to the assigned fundraiser in a timely manner, the assigned fundraiser can use this information as a springboard to reach out, congratulate and further move the prospect along the solicitation cycle ultimately leading to a gift.

Actionable Intelligence is one of the key drivers of all things *Precision Prospect Development.* It will have the greatest ROI of anything you can do. Make sure to focus on this and master this concept. ***For everything that***

you do, and everything that your program produces, works on, and/or pushes out to your constituents - always - run it by the actionable intelligence litmus test. Ask yourself – is this actionable? **Is this going to prompt some sort of action by the recipient and/or get them closer to taking the next best action at the right time?** If the answer is no, then nine out of ten times it is not worth doing. In order to fine-tune the activities of your program for maximum impact, you must utilize the actionable intelligence litmus test.

Prospect Development is in the position to help create and set the direction of activities on both the micro and macro levels within an organization. Through operating under the direction of actionable intelligence you will be able to set great wheels into motion. Through proper focus and dissemination of actionable intelligence you can help your organization double-or even triple-fundraising revenue.

As your actionable intelligence begins to drive and impact revenue, fundraisers and senior leadership will take notice. Your reputation will grow. Demand for your services, presence, and input will increase. Your relationships with your constituents will improve, and as your relationships improve, the impact of your work will increase. You'll know more about your constituents. The more you know about your constituents the more you can apply *Precision Prospect Development* to deliver custom-tailored work. The more precise your work, the more efficiency you'll create; your repertoire will expand. You'll get more, higher-level, and higher-visibility projects.

As you get more and higher-visibility projects, you'll get access to more data about your organization and its strategies. The more you know your organization's priorities, strategies and inner workings, the more precisely you can plug into the DNA of your organization and align your activities accordingly. With more exposure to fundraisers and senior leadership, you'll get more insight into how things work at the higher level. When you reach this level, you deliver even more impactful actionable intelligence. You'll have a seat at the table. Your value will become self-evident. Your department's fingerprints will be all over the gifts and there will be no doubt about your position in the chain of cause and effect. You'll get more access to resources because the ROI will be irrefutable.

As you get more in-sync with your shop and build better and closer relationships with fundraisers, you'll get to learn more about fundraising from the fundraiser perspective. This will allow you to begin to think more and more like an actual fundraiser. This will also align your shop closer to the gift so that you can begin to start practicing bottom-line *Precision Prospect Development.*

Actionable Intelligence is the guide that I've successfully built two Prospect Development shops around. I've witnessed the above chain of events happen first-hand at two separate organizations. If you are the leader of the Prospect Development program, you must constantly ask your team about what impact they see a certain project having and why. You must use the actionable intelligence litmus test. If there is no action that can be taken from the project then you should explore a little more, ask why, and make sure that it is worth doing. Through this exploration, you can better prioritize and remove projects from the queue.

Examine your past work and look for what prompted action by your fundraisers. You may even have to get so granular as to understand exactly what each individual fundraiser takes action on. Observe what this is and give them more of it. Remove that which does not prompt action by your fundraisers and focus your effort on that which does.

In addition to observing, you can embark on a series of one-on-one interviews with your fundraisers to learn what they take action on. Engage in conversations and ask what they are looking for that will help them to increase positive activity. Take note of what they say, and put it into practice. Make sure to monitor the results though to ensure that they gave you the right data. Actions speak louder than words.

Implement more actionable intelligence for greater success. Prompting action through data is one of the highest forms of success for *Precision Prospect Development.* When our work does not prompt action, we need to examine it further and find out why. If no one takes action on our data, we can't have an impact.

Chapter 10

If No One Uses It, It can't have an Impact

"If a tree falls in the forest and no one is around to hear it, does it make a sound?"

Unknown, Philosophy Question

Studying philosophy in college, I encountered this question quite a bit. I heard it ad naseum and almost found it to be a rather silly question to ponder. Now that I have been working in the Prospect Development field for over ten years, I find that this question highlights one of the most valuable concepts we can learn in our field. If you can master this concept and guide your business strategy around it, you will greatly increase your impact at your organization. Remember, our goal is to drive action through delivering actionable intelligence that leads to more/better engagement with donors/prospects that results in more revenue. Inaction is therefore one of our biggest adversaries that we must overcome. Our work is action-oriented. ***When our work does not lead to action, we are not doing our work. The key word is action.***

When translated to our business setting, this question can be asked as such: *If you completed project x and no one looked at it or used it, did it happen/does it exist?* The answer is this: *If it was not used by your stakeholder, then it essentially does not exist.* If it does not exist to your stakeholder and the entire reason for completing it is to benefit your stakeholder, then we must ask ourselves "Why did we complete it?" We must take a step back and look a little bit deeper at the variables involved and ensure that we don't repeat this pattern in the future at too high frequency.

With *Actionable Intelligence* as one of your key drivers, you don't want to waste any of your limited time working on projects or building business systems that are not going to get looked at or used. If no one uses them, they can't have an impact or bring more dollars in the door; they can't further your organization's mission. They can't create new efficiencies for your stakeholders, or optimize the donor experience. Use this perennial philosophical question as your measuring stick to determine if you should do a project. Think about who is going to use it and for what end. If you determine that it is going to be used, understanding the end goals can help to determine how many resources to allocate to the project as well as to know when to start and when to finish.

You're not always going to know what is going to have the greatest impact, and you can't guarantee that everything you do will be used. You can, however, greatly increase the probability of knowing what will be useful through paying attention to the past and tuning into the present. Learn from past projects and follow up with your stakeholders to determine what got used and how. Find out what didn't get used and why. You can use this information to further refine your projects, so that you cut out more of the elements that have less likelihood of being helpful, and increase the elements that have a higher likelihood of being helpful. Have open and honest communication with your stakeholders so that they can be open about what is and is not working for them. Make sure that you are in a position where they will tell you when something is not working, or that they didn't look at it and why.

Make sure you have a solid understanding of what they can absorb and take on at any given moment. Often the reason for a project falling through the cracks is bandwidth; when this is the case then you can understand that the issue is delivery method and timing. You'll need to refine the timing of your delivery and your method to have the highest chance of success. This might mean shortening an email from three paragraphs to a few bullet points and timing it so that it will get read and get the key information across.

Make sure you have a solid understanding of your stakeholders' competencies. Through understanding what they are able to comprehend, you can custom your deliverables to match their current state. When the issue is competency, you will have to change up variables around complexity and ease of use to ensure the highest chance of success.

Sometimes your project will need an adjustment to land if it didn't land at first. Some projects are not worth giving up on, but just need a little more time or a different approach to be successful. When one of your projects falls through the cracks, analyze the data around why, and the results will help determine the proper path to ensure success; if the results of your analysis determine that, an alternative approach is deemed necessary.

Make sure that you are actively engaging your stakeholders in the present moment. Learn as much as you can about what is happening right now. Find out what their current needs are and what their future needs might be. Learn as much as you can about your organization. Spend time observing the present state. Get plugged into your organization's DNA, and make sure that your work is informed by the past, aligned with the present, and facing the future.

Operate your business in this fashion and I guarantee that the majority of your work will be actionable, will impact the bottom line, and will increase efficiency. Apply the strategies and tactics outlined in this book and you will be able to master all of these concepts and your work will not fall on deaf ears. Everything is connected, and through exploring the vast layers between project and outcome, you will refine and distill down your workflow to achieve the highest balance of action inducing output.

Chapter 11

INTERCONNECTEDNESS

It only takes a small shift in perspective to go from me to we.

Have you ever thought about how everything in the cosmos and beyond is interconnected? If you think about this concept, it is actually a pretty amazing and overwhelming thing. Put your toe in any ocean on the planet and you are connected, by water, to the entire globe. Jump in and swim and you are swimming with the continents. An American swimming in a beach in Santa Monica, California, is swimming in the same water as an Indian across the globe in Kerala, India. Kneel down and place your hand on a road in the United States and you are connected to each and every point of all roads on the mainland. Step on the earth and you are connected to everyone and everything that is touching the ground. Take off your shoes and connect. ***Know that we are all more similar than we are dissimilar and that our points of connection to each other and to the universe are endless.***

Understand and master the concept of interconnection. The more you are able to grasp this concept, the further you will be able to see and understand impact and the more you will be able to understand cause and effect; the more you will see areas of synergy within your office, your activities and with colleagues; the more you are able to identify and harness synergy, you will be able to apply and create efficiencies. The more efficiency you create, the more you will be able to do. The more you are able to do, the greater your impact. The greater your impact, the more money your organization will raise. The more money your organization raises, the greater the potential positive impact on the planet; you will be given more resources, and the cycle continues. ***Positive impact on the planet increases exponentially.***

Watch for interconnection in your workflow and harness synergy wherever you discover ideal intersections of interconnection. Follow things to their logical conclusion. Understand how your work connects to the values of your organization and set the course for maximum impact. Tune into the DNA of your organizational culture, mission and values and connect your activity accordingly.

Precision Prospect Development is all about harnessing the interconnectedness of all things in an organization. We are one of the only programs positioned to touch each and every unit in development since we work closely with all departments. Through our working relationships, we come to learn their business models, goals, strategies, and current projects. This is such a huge advantage, especially when silos are an ever present threat to the success of every organization. Conversely, this is also a big responsibility. We must use our connectedness within the organization to increase the connectedness of our organizational culture to break down silos.

As you work with different departments and notice overlaps in projects between different teams, always do your best to connect the dots and connect the teams. Through connecting these dots and getting the teams together, you help to uncover blind spots and help ensure that the donor experience is not disrupted or thrown off course. You will often stop big mishaps from happening, and will create efficiencies, reduce costs, and reduce duplication of effort. You will also get brought more into the loop on each department's activities because they will easily see the value of plugging their activity into your platform. When you operate in this manner, you actually add an additional type of actionable intelligence that is highly valuable: *internal actionable intelligence*, when you deliver overlapping or vital information about the activities of an individual or group to another individual or group within your organization.

Your value as a silo buster will not go unnoticed. This proactive step goes a long way with leadership. There is nothing worse than a non-profit organization that crisscrosses messages with donors in a way that disrupts the donor experience. When a donor experience is disrupted it can cost your organization anything from bad feelings to actual losses of millions of dollars in revenue. Remember that the optimization of the donor experience is of vital importance.

Chapter 12

MASTER DISTILLERS

"Sit and drink Pennyroyal Tea, ***Distill*** the life that's inside of me"

Kurt Cobain, Nirvana
Pennyroyal Tea

I attended graduate school at Hebrew College in Newton, MA, where I studied Philosophy and Biblical Hebrew. All we did was read and write papers. There were never any tests, just a lot of writing. My favorite professor was Rabbi Nehemia Polen, who taught classes in Jewish mystical thought, in particular, Hasidism. On one occasion, a few days after we had turned in our latest writing assignment, he held up our graded papers in his hand and said "Ok, look everybody. First off, I appreciate all of your hard work that went into writing these. However, what I am holding in my hands here is a bunch of sap. I don't want sap. What I want is maple syrup. We are in New England, so you all should understand this analogy. In order to make a gallon of maple syrup, it requires 40 gallons of sap. You have to distill down the sap so that it can turn into maple syrup. Stop giving me sap. I don't want to read all of that. I want you to continue refining your content and distill it down ever further to its essence, and instead of giving me, say, 20-25 pages of sap, give me 5 pages of syrup. Get to the heart of your thesis faster. Choose your words wisely. Reread your papers, and if the content is not necessary for your argument, remove it."

Distillation is hard work. ***In order to distill the complex down into simple parts it requires an intimate knowledge of the complex.*** Professor Polen knew this, and pushed us to work hard at grasping the higher concepts we were studying and then fine tune the art of translating them back through the arguments in our papers with precision and simplicity. This is precisely why we must get plugged into the DNA of our organizations through an intimate awareness and understanding of the interplay of the *six elements* in all things. This is why we must have an intimate knowledge of the fundraising process, each department's activities in our shop and Prospect Development as a whole. We need this mastery of knowledge in order to have a shot at mastering the distillation process, leaving behind what is unnecessary, and leaving in only the essential ingredients.

Professor Polen didn't have time to read through all that sap. It was too inefficient and our theses were drowning in seas of unnecessary words. Attention spans are only getting shorter. People are not able to filter through vast amounts of information like they once could. ***The skill of distillation is of the utmost importance now if you want your end user to understand and take action on the information you are presenting to them.*** We are the filters and our output should be nicely-packaged, refined, efficient data products that get to the point quickly. Cut too much, and your message is lost; include too much, and your message is lost. *Balance is key.*

Precision Prospect Development is all about mastering the distillation process. We are master distillers of data and business processes. We are all faced with three of the same common dilemmas. The first distillation dilemma asks: How can we best reconcile the fact that we have unlimited data, possibilities, and prospects, combined with limited resources, staff, and time? How can we identify the best prospects for each fundraising unit at the right time, and match them with the right opportunity that will unlock their giving potential to its maximum level of output? How do we set up a system to not only find needles in a haystack, but to find a purple needle, a blue needle, a green needle, or a needle that matches best with any current need? How do we take all of the data that we have on our prospects and take all of the data that we have on our organization and end up with unique *programmatic pathways* for each prospect in the database?

There is only one way. Master the art of data distillation through the science of data mining, analytics, algorithms, machine learning, artificial intelligence and human intelligence. Take those mountains of data and turn them into actionable intelligence that is aligned with your organization's makeup and mission, always providing the right balance and timing so as to increase effectiveness and success. Use this actionable intelligence to optimize the donor experience as much as possible.

We can solve this distillation dilemma most efficiently through the creation of a *Precision Philanthropy Platform.* Answer one question at a time. The combination of questions and answers will act as the foundation for our platform.[9] We must distill down massive amounts of data with the use of analytics run by a mix of the human mind asking the right questions, and providing the proper guidance, blended with machine learning/artificial intelligence. The result will be actionable intelligence in its purest form for fundraising staff. We will have to abandon the static models of yesterday, and create living models that get smarter over time and change as data changes.

The second distillation dilemma we face deals with internal mechanics and processes. We have a lot of activities that we perform, but they might not all be worth doing. We need to apply the principle of distillation to our own functions and the function of our department.

---

[9] See Chapter 15 "The Platform" and Chapter 27 "Decision Tree" for more on this.

Distill your project load down so that you are not engaging in repetitive tasks. We need to make sure that each and every activity or project that we work on is the right one that will have the highest ROI at that time. ***We must make sure that all we do is somehow having an impact on the bottom-line, the donor experience and/or furthering our organization's mission in the best possible way.*** We must fine tune our workflow to maximize efficiency and automate as many of the repetitive processes as possible. We must use the litmus tests of *actionable intelligence* and *project value* to ensure that all activities are in alignment with our organization's DNA.

The third distillation dilemma has to do with our projects and communications. We must make sure that our projects and communications are properly distilled prior to dissemination. Too complex and you will lose your audience, too simple and you might not be getting deep enough. Balance is important. Play to your audience; distill the information contained in each project and communication so that they are digestible. Often you can manage your workload in a way where you do less but achieve more.

In addition to pointing the act of distillation outwardly to your work and function, also think about how to do this from within. Perfect the workings of your own internal refinery; burn off the irrelevant noise and only allow pure product to pour out. Your output will increase and so will your productivity and impact.

If we are ever to show how truly valuable our data is, we must convert it from its raw state into a more valuable form through the distillation and refinement processes. We must mine through the data and find the precious metals, burn off the impurities, and forge them into revenue-generating bits of actionable insight.

Chapter 13

DATA AS AN ASSET (INFONOMICS)

"*Infonomics:* The emerging discipline of managing and accounting for information with the same or similar rigor and formality as other traditional assets (e.g. financial, physical, intangible, human capital). Infonomics posits that information itself meets all the criteria of formal company assets, and, although not yet recognized by generally accepted accounting practices, increasingly, it is incumbent on organizations to behave as if it were to optimize information's ability to generate business value."

Gartner IT Glossary

Demonstrating the value of data to your organization is key to getting a seat at the table while unlocking additional resources and responsibilities for you and your team. This concept as defined by Gartner is surprisingly a relatively new one, but it has really taken off in the past few years and is increasingly more and more becoming common knowledge in the for-profit sector. We still have a lot of work to go in making this common knowledge through which strategies are designed and derived to take advantage of this asset.

Let's do a little thought experiment:

Take out a pad of paper and take a moment and think and jot down what you think are the top assets are at your organization. What are the top assets for your non-profit organization? Or for any non-profit organization?

When I ponder this question, the five that come to mind are as follows:

1. People (Employees, Donors, Volunteers, etc.)
2. Endowment
3. Brand
4. Mission
5. **Data**

Can you think of any more at your organization?

Did you know that all of these top assets form an ecosystem in which they all work synergistically together? This means that a strength in any one asset strengthens all of the others; a weakness in any asset weakens all of the others. If we don't treat our data like the asset it is and invest in it, then that means that the value of our people, endowment, brand and mission will all suffer as a result. It is vital that each non-profit invest in all of their assets so that they can reach their fullest potential and provide maximum benefit to the world through the fulfillment their missions. This means that the proper attention and investment must be made in the area of data, especially if we are to maximize revenue.

The for-profit sector figured out that data is an asset a long time ago.

They have been maximizing the value of their data for decades. In the tech sector, a majority of the recent company acquisitions have taken place because the purchasing company wants the *data* of the company being purchased more so than their products or services. In fact, the value of most company's data far exceeds that of their core products or services that they provide.

If you look even deeper, you will discover that there are quite a few companies out there that are actually data-capturing companies that operate under the guise of providing a product or service, when in reality, data collection is their core product and highest valued asset. If a company's data holds the key to unlocking some insight or additional revenue by another company, then they are likely to become an acquisition target. We are talking trillions of dollars in market capitalization here. Trillions.

Back in 2014 I found myself having a conversation with my newly-appointed manager, and I was trying to prove how valuable our data was, and trying to pitch the case for a more structured and scientific approach to data collection and database usage. After I was able to get him to agree that our data was an asset, I asked, ***"If data is an asset, then why do we treat our database like a liability?"***

This unplanned outburst set me off on this path of trying to get non-profits to understand the value of their data, and figure out how to best extract and display that value. Think about that question. Ask that question to your senior leadership if you are facing this same problem of not having folks buy into the importance of database participation. If data is an asset, then our databases are actually worth anywhere from tens, to hundreds of millions, to potentially billions of dollars. This is huge. When leadership understands this, they tend to look at things a little differently and can go from being disengaged and disinterested to engaged, passionate backers of creating a more data driven culture. Remember that at the end of the day, the bottom line tends to have the most sway, especially the higher up you go in the hierarchy of your organization. Bottom-line thinking should always be at the top of your mind.

Data as an asset means that we must take it seriously. We must invest in our data verses. Our data should be front and center on the minds of senior leadership. We need to hire more data scientists. Data as an asset means that the more we collect, ensure accuracy, run analytics, etc., the more value we will be able to extract from our data. This will, in turn, increase the value our data. This sets in motion a value creation chain of events with our data. As the value of our data increases, we are able to extract more value from our data. The more value we can extract from our data, the more our leadership will allot for investment in our data, the more we invest, the more we can extract.

Always remember that a well-oiled *Precision Prospect Development* machine will not only generate more revenue per fundraiser, but will also allow for more fundraisers to be hired to generate even more revenue. Revenue is generated through providing top notch donor experiences and matching donors with the proper programmatic pathways. Ponder this: ***The basis of our data work lies in how data is captured, organized, accessed and analyzed.***

Data as an asset also means that if neglected or underutilized, the value decreases. If we don't take it seriously, or don't make the appropriate investments, it will be of little value and we won't be able to use our data to generate much revenue. Poor investment and maintenance of data leads to the belief that data is not valuable. Some leaders at broken shops might cite this as a reason to not invest. Don't allow this to happen to you.

Fortunately for us, big data is such a buzzword these days that most folks are becoming more and more hip to the value of data. The Economist published an article in the summer of 2017 that argues that data is now the world's most-valuable asset.[10] The tide is changing in our favor. Ride this wave of big data, and make sure that you and your organization are not undervaluing one of your most-valued assets.

[10] "The world's most valuable resource is no longer oil, but data" *The Economist*, May 6th 2017

Ask the following questions about your current situation and allow the answers to guide your strategies on what to do next to ensure that you are able to implement a data-drive culture:

- Does your organization currently view its data as an asset or a liability?
- Does leadership take your organization's data seriously and make data-driven decisions?
- Does your organization invest the appropriate amount of resources in your dataverse?
- Does your organization have a data strategy or data philosophy?
- Is there a VP or AVP directly in charge of your data who understands its importance and value?

Chapter 14

DATA PHILOSOPHY

"We the people… in Order to form a more perfect Union,
establish Justice, ensure domestic Tranquility,
provide for the common defense, promote the general Welfare,
and secure the Blessings of Liberty to ourselves and our Posterity"

United States Constitution

Does your organization have a data philosophy? Do you have a set of guiding principles that drive how you manage, maintain, access and utilize data? Does each employee at your organization take ownership over their data and ensure accuracy and timeliness of input? Does each employee know what is expected of them with regards to data? If you answered no to any of these questions, you might want to consider writing a data philosophy.

A data philosophy can work wonders for your organization. A data philosophy helps to set the tone and shape the culture around data; it provides the overall structure and guiding principles of how data is to be regarded. It can answer all of the questions asked above and more.

A data philosophy creates visibility at all levels in your organization around your data. It can surface and bring to light how vital, valuable and important your data is to success. It can provide you with the necessary backing to implement office-wide systems that increase data quality and quantity. It shows that senior leadership is paying attention and taking this matter seriously.

Your data is an asset that must be managed appropriately and in proportion to its value. You must have some policies and procedures around how you capture and manage data if you are going to increase and maximize the value. A data philosophy ensures that you are setting up the proper guidelines to help increase the value of your data at a high level.

When I joined the City of Hope, I made it a priority to work on and disseminate our data philosophy to help guide our office through the transition of becoming a data-driven culture. My team created a business card that captured our data philosophy, with a button attached along with the logo of our CRM system. We handed them out to everyone in our office at a meeting to help promote the vision captured in the philosophy. We give them to new employees now as a part of their onboarding.

Data Philosophy Template:

[Insert Organization Name] places a premium on the collection and maintenance of data. We understand that a strong data-centric organization enhances our ability to make informed decisions and build effective strategies that will best impact our ability to support the mission of [Insert Organization Name] and provide the ultimate donor experience. [Insert Organization Name] is committed to applying the appropriate resources necessary to ensure that our data is robust, reliable, accessible and secure.

Chapter 15

THE PLATFORM

Complexity is the combination of multiple simplicities.

The Platform is a series of interconnected systems blended together, utilizing artificial intelligence technologies (machine learning, natural language processing, etc.) to push out actionable intelligence to team members in order to increase revenue, forward the mission of an organization and optimize the donor experience. *The Platform* breathes life into your data so that it can talk back and tell us about each and every constituent in the database and what to do with each of them at any given time. It is plugged into all of your various data sources so that you can have as complete and holistic of a picture as possible. It relies on living models and segments of one.[11]

Begin building your platform by solving your most-pressing need. Once you have done this, move on to the next pressing need, and so on

[11] See Chapter 16 "The Living Model" and Chapter 17 "The Segment of One"

and so forth. You will end up with a complex cybernetic structure that is the aggregate of many simple systems. *The Platform* is like a forest made up of multiple interconnected decision trees. My recommendation on where to begin building your platform is in chapter 27, "Decision Tree".

The programmatic pathways are our solutions to our pressing needs. A *programmatic pathway* is a tailored approach that addresses the uniqueness of each individual or group in the constituent base and shapes the approach to match the uniqueness in any given environment and for any given desired outcome. It is made up of *next-best actions.*

If you are not yet ready to deploy artificial intelligence technologies, that is ok, you can still prepare yourself by implementing all of the strategies outlined in this book and building some basic algorithms. If you implement these strategies, you will be ready to plug into the machines when they are more readily available, and/or affordable or accessible.

For most of us, the base of our platforms are our data warehouses. This is where we can connect multiple data sources and utilize basic software/code to blend them together. We are not going to get too technical here, as your technique will rely mostly on your organization's specifics. The bottom line is this: your platform is at the base of your raw data. It is the place where all of your data sources can come together. It will require some programming and/or software to get insight from your blended data. This is where either an old fashioned algorithm or some machine learning comes into play. More important than this, though, is having a problem to solve.

If you cannot do anything else, at least you can collect more data. Track your organization's activities. Make sure you have as many samples or examples as possible of behaviors, outcomes, prospects, etc., so that you can get the most out of your platform. This data will serve you, and the earlier you begin, the process of collecting more relevant data on your organization's and prospects' activities, the easier it will be to translate that into actionable insight through machine learning when it becomes available to you. Remember, complexity is built on a mountain of simplicities.

Chapter 16

THE LIVING MODEL

As our data changes, so too should our strategies.

If you asked a friend if they could help you to cross the street safely, and they gave you a picture of the intersection from the month prior and said this will get you across safely, would you trust that picture and the placement of the cars in the photograph to guide you safely through the intersection? The chances of the cars in the photo aligning with the current state of the placement and motion of cars is almost 0%.

If you wanted to know what the skyline of Seattle looked like, and someone gave you a picture from five years ago filled with cranes putting up new buildings, would you trust that photo to accurately represent the current skyline?

Would you buy a house only based on pictures that were three years old? Would you trust that the structure hadn't changed significantly enough to affect the value? Would you trust that the house was still standing?

If you wanted to survey the landscape of a forest to determine how many trees were available for timber production and you were given a satellite image from one year ago, would you feel confident putting in a bid to buy the timberland based on what appeared to be available then?

Like me, you probably answered no to all of the above questions. If so, then why would you pay for a static model that does not allow for updates as your data changes? Why would you purchase something that promises to predict the propensity of a prospect in the here and now that cannot take into effect the changing variables?

Prospects are constantly shifting and can go from not a viable prospect to a viable prospect in an instant and then back again to not viable. Timing is so important in fundraising and windows of opportunity open and close all around us constantly. Our ability to successfully get through as many open opportunities as possible will be the differentiator between success and super success. We must ensure that we have tools that can operate on this level and can take into account the changing landscape that we are faced with.

What if our predictive models were alive, were self-correcting, learned from their results, and constantly evolved? What if they gave feedback on how they performed, and adjusted to the presence or absence of data elements in any given record? What if they were able to apply different aspects of the features in different ways depending upon the uniqueness of each individual? As we move into the era of *Precision Prospect Development*, we will cast away the static model of old in favor of the living, malleable model.

Through the integration of machine learning into our platform, we will breathe life into our models and achieve even greater results. The models will grow more precise and sharper over time, and, in turn, increase effectiveness. Gone will be the days of purchasing a static model from an organization and updating it every few years. In fact, we will soon look back on this and wonder how we ever operated in this manner. We will wonder how we crossed the street safely with the sole guidance of a photograph of the intersection and not get struck by a moving vehicle. Ten years from now, machine learning will be an aspect of all of our models.

The nature of the world is *change*, as is the nature of our datasets and our constituent base. As things in the life of a prospect evolve and change, so do their philanthropic priorities. If what was true in the morning will become a lie in the evening, then the only way to operate a predictive model is to utilize machine learning. With machine learning becoming more and more accessible, it will become more adopted in the non-profit sector. This can be done in-house. It sounds more complicated than it actually is. The important thing is to make sure that you are collecting and tracking as much data as possible so that you are ready for the AI revolution when it arrives at your door.

Chapter 17

THE SEGMENT OF ONE

Generalities do not exist. There is no they. There is only I.

Precision Prospect Development is all about the distillation of data into actionable intelligence that is precisely pinpointed to match prospects with a programmatic pathway. A *programmatic pathway* is a tailored approach that addresses the uniqueness of each individual or group in the constituent base and shapes the approach to match the uniqueness in any given environment and for any given desired outcome. A programmatic pathway is lined with *next best action*s that lead to the desired outcome. This is like a decision tree, where the specific data of each prospect determines the *next best action* that is taken at any given time. There is no one size fits all or no model that will dictate what to do to everyone to achieve the best overall results.

Modeling looks for patterns. It groups people together based on similarities in lifestyle, belief, and behaviors. It can create a grouping that includes millions of folks and can give them the same score. With machine learning, we have the opportunity to create micro segments down to a segment of one; we can hone in on one prospect or a small group of prospects and have a strategy so precise that it is unique to that individual or small group. I was at a conference not too long ago and there was a panel of data experts. A question came up about modeling. One of the panelists announced with great authority, "We did some sentiment analysis to see if sending a handwritten thank you note would impact giving, and while it was relevant for some people, it didn't make very much of a difference for a majority of people. Therefore it is not statistically relevant to send handwritten thank you notes so you shouldn't do it."

I hear statements like this all of the time and find them very peculiar. When I heard this I thought, 'What about the population where it does make a difference?' Once you find out who it does positively affect, isolate that group and make sure that they receive handwritten notes. Let's keep our machine learning running this sentiment analysis and add people to the group and take folks out of the group as necessary. ***If something works for someone, then it should be applied to that someone, not ignored because it doesn't work for everyone.*** Even if your data indicates that something is relevant for even just one person in your dataset then why not implement for that person?

With our *Precision Prospect Development* platform, we are not looking for one size fits all solutions, or the best thing to do to your entire population to get the most results. ***We are looking to create multiple micro segments that result in what are essentially segments of one so that the pathway for each prospect is uniquely tailored to them.*** One person may get a certain ad on social media, two mailings per year of a certain card stock with an individualized message, or a phone call after their gifts. ***Using data modeling to find who will respond best to each of your outreach methods, you will gradually customize more and more each prospect's experience, further refining your organization's approach until you have reached the most effective and personalized approach.***[12]

[12] See chapter 27 "Decision Tree"

We want to scale the activities of fundraisers so that we can apply a personalized experience to as many people as possible in our databases. This is really the whole point of our cybernetic structure, to extend everyone's reach and capabilities. Remember, we have limited fundraisers with limited time, but seemingly unlimited prospects. Through modeling in this fashion, we can increase the reach of our fundraisers exponentially and bubble up more warm-hot prospects at the right time for an even more personalized experience.

In order to achieve this, we must understand fundraising and fundraisers as much as possible and take complete stock of our organization's available resources, its structure, the available methods of outreach and possible ways of interacting with prospects. This will all be readily available to you as you grow more and more intimately aware and connected to the DNA of your organization and the *six elements* that underlie its existence.

Chapter 18

STATISTICAL RELEVANCE

Maximize your use of statistics so that they benefit everyone in your database.

I think that we need to re-evaluate how we approach statistical relevancy and modeling in this new age of *Precision Prospect Development.* We impart analytics so that we don't use the old strategy of simply throwing spaghetti against the wall and seeing what sticks; we impart analytics to get as precise as possible with our activities and interactions surrounding our donors. ***We want to reach as many people as possible with the highest degree of personalization while choosing the best possible methods at the right time.*** This does not mean that we want to find what works best with most of the folks in our prospect base and apply to all. This means that we want to find what works the best for each and every one of the folks in our prospect base and apply at scale on an individual level. ***We don't want a better way to throw spaghetti against the wall; we want to find a way to serve our prospects their favorite meals.***

Don't get me wrong. Traditional models are valuable and have proven to help increase efficiency in a myriad of ways. They are still valuable and will still help your organization to increase efficiency. However, we now have some additional technology that can take those static models and breathe life into them so that they can operate in a much more precise manner.

As we embark on the age of AI, why would we want to only run large models that apply to the broadest of populations, or a static model that doesn't learn? If these are the only models that we are undertaking, then we are going to miss the mark more and more. We are not taking advantage of the technology that is out there in today's market already being utilized by for-profit corporations.

When looking for and applying statistical relevance, we need to ask, "To whom is this statistically relevant? To which records would making a change in this area have an impact?" The answer might be on more of a micro-level rather than a macro-level.

Our modeling has to take both the macro and micro approach if we are to squeeze out every bit of value that we have in our datasets. We have to use the kind of modeling technology that allows for macro observations to be applied with precision on a 1:1 scale. Meaning build one machine learning model that has the ability to be applied in an infinite number of ways across your population so that it finds the precise formula within the model to apply to each individual record. A model that looks at statistical relevance and reinvents its application to our data and strategies that we take with prospects.

Chapter 19

THINK LIKE A FUNDRAISER

We are all fundraisers.

In order to truly deliver precision, custom, amazing fundraising products, you have to think like a fundraiser. In order to think like a fundraiser, you'll have to learn as much as you can about fundraising and put yourself in the shoes of a fundraiser. If you don't know what it is like to solicit a gift, how can you be sure that what you are providing as support is what is truly needed? If you don't engage with your fundraisers, how can you learn what they need in order to help propel them to success?

Often at Prospect Development conferences, I hear about the struggles of researchers and data scientists in dealing with fundraisers and how "if only the fundraisers would do this or that, then things would go much better. They could raise more money." Whenever I hear this, I always have the same reply: "Do you ever communicate what you would like them to do? Or ask what they need from you in order to be able to move forward? Do you ever ask them what success looks like? Do you know their goals, and provide them with the actionable intelligence necessary for them to exceed their goals?"

On the other side of the fence, whenever I attend conferences with fundraisers, I hear a completely different side of the story. Fundraisers usually complain to me that "If only I could get my researchers to do this or that then things would go much better. I could raise more money." One particular example was a fundraiser who said, "I only want to know where their largest gift was but they give me everything but that." Whenever I have these conversations, I always have the same reply: "Do you ever communicate what you would like them to do? Or ask them what they need to know in order to get you what you want so that you can move forward? Do you share your goals with them? Do you talk about ideal state, what info you like to see and what characteristics you are looking for to get you excited to take on a new prospect?"

Almost every time I ask these questions, the answer is invariably a resounding "No." To which I reply, "How do you expect to get in sync with each other if you are not communicating? If you can communicate this to someone you met at a conference, surely you can communicate it with your colleagues."

In order to think like a fundraiser, you must first get to know your fundraisers. You will never know what they need if you don't understand who they are as people, what they are tasked with accomplishing in their role, and how they go about accomplishing their tasks. You will never know what they want if you don't know who they are, how they learn, absorb information, what kind of data they like to see, how they like spreadsheets formatted, what makes them get excited.

Meet individually with your fundraisers to get to know them and forge solid bonds. Don't be afraid to put yourself out there. Invite them out to lunch. Meet them for happy hour after work. Begin each meeting you have with them talking about common, shared interests. Engage with them on an individual, personal level. Learn about their passions. Find out how they really feel. Find out what they really want, and deliver precisely that. Find out what keeps them up at night about their work. Find out what causes them stress and what makes them feel satisfied or successful. Build that rapport so that they can come to you and communicate open and honestly knowing that there is a foundation of trust and shared notion of responsibility in success.

When you deliver a product or project or spreadsheet, don't just send it in an email and forget about it. Deliver it in person, or follow-up in person after you send it to walk them through it, and/or solicit feedback. When you walk them through it, pay attention to what they pay attention to. Find out what they liked about the product, what features they found most useful, what features they could do without. Take this feedback and incorporate it into refining your work moving forward. Over time, your work will become more and more precisely distilled and honed in on their needs and this will result in more success. You'll spend less time on each request and have more time to deliver more actionable intelligence.

It is ironic that we as researchers have a natural inclination to profile people and determine likelihood to do a certain action like make a gift, yet we can remain clueless about who our fundraisers are and what they need for success. Or we neglect to incorporate our data on our fundraisers into our methods of working with them. ***Use this analytical talent to profile your fundraisers and determine who likes what and who reacts to certain information a certain way and customize your behavior based on this information.*** Deliver precision reports based on this information. It will save you time, increase your ratio of success, build better relationships, increase efficiency and increase effectiveness.

Fundraising is hard work. In addition to getting to know your fundraisers, it is vital that you also get to know fundraising. Learn as much about being a fundraiser as you can. Learn about fundraising in general and learn about what fundraisers in your shop do. Instead of attending a Prospect Development conference one year, attend a conference specifically meant for front line fundraisers. You might learn more on how to be an effective Prospect Development professional at a fundraising conference than at a research/data conference. Purchase some books on front-line fundraising, read articles, attend webinars on raising gifts, and set up informational meetings with your field staff. The more you can immerse yourself in the world of raising gifts, the more you will be filled with ideas on how to best support through the use of data and actionable intelligence.

The more you know about what it is like to be a fundraiser, the more you can fine tune your research and to look for patterns that relate to what a fundraiser wants and needs. The more you know about your particular fundraisers, the more you can customize your research to propel them forward and provide them with the information and tools to exceed their goals.

One of the key elements to learning about the activities of your fundraisers is their goals. Find out what your fundraiser's goals are and refer to them often. Knowing their goals is key. At Stanford, I used to start out each year with a meeting with each fundraising unit I supported, along with each individual I supported to find out what their goals were for the year. I would use this information to guide the activities of my shop and refer to this information throughout the year to keep on course.

I learned information in these meetings that I never would have known had I not asked or had a good enough rapport with my fundraisers. The data gathered through learning about goals set the course for my shop for the year, and allowed for the prioritization of projects to match up with the goals of the organization. With some departments that I worked close with, we would actually go so far as to share draft goals with each other and build goals around each other that complimented each other. This pre-sharing and working together on goals is the ideal state.

Make sure to incorporate all you learn about the goals of your constituents into your actionable intelligence litmus test. As you come up with team projects, make sure they are supportive of, and in line with, the goals of your fundraisers. You will be surprised at how many projects you can think of that can support the goals of your constituents once you know what they are. In fact, you will likely think of some great ideas at the exact same time that you are meeting with your constituents.

You might even want to take on a small portfolio of a handful of prospects for a specified period of time. This will really show you what it takes to be a fundraiser. You'll get a first-hand taste of the challenges and absorb a ton of data on the fundraising process that you can take back and incorporate into your work.

By learning about fundraising, learning about the goals and activities of fundraisers in your organization, and through personally getting to know your fundraisers, you will empower yourself with all the tools necessary to provide the most actionable, bottom-line-driven products that will have your organization breaking fundraising goals. Yes, that's right, breaking fundraising goals.

Chapter 20

Focus on the Bottom Line: Prospect Development as Revenue Generator

What kind of value is this project going to add?
Is this the value that is most needed and/or valued by the organization?

Project Value Litmus Test

Precision Prospect Development sets its sights on the bottom line and remains hyper focused on impact to the bottom line. ***Bottom line thinking is always at the top of mind*** for senior leadership. This should also be the case in Prospect Development. Shift your focus so that bottom line thinking is always top of mind. ***We are revenue generators.***

How are we revenue generators you may ask? We are revenue generators in two major ways:

1. ***The activities of a Prospect Development department allow for more revenue to be generated per fundraiser***

2. ***The activities of a Prospect Development department allow for more fundraisers to be hired to generate revenue.***

In addition to being revenue generators there is one additional key way in which Prospect Development impacts the bottom-line:

1. ***The activities of a Prospect Development department allow for efficiencies to be created so that more can be done with less resources.***

2. ***The activities of a Prospect Development department allow for efficiencies to be created so that more value can be extracted from current resources.***

Is your current focus ensuring that this is taking place to its fullest potential? Think about these four outcomes that impact the bottom-line. Is your department dedicated to conducting projects that will have the greatest impact in one of these four areas or another area that is directly tied to the bottom-line? ***Remember that revenue generated is almost always valued over and above efficiencies related to cost savings.***

The most important goal for a fundraiser is dollars in the door. Always remember this. At the end of the day, this is usually the most important of all goals in a philanthropy organization. The more you help your fundraisers nail this, the more resources you will receive to do your job. The more resources you have, the more you can do, thus creating a cycle of abundance and ensuring the success of your role, department, and organization. Therefore, you must think of your projects from a bottom-line perspective. Think of how you allocate your resources and how you spend your time. If a project fails the litmus test of adding value to the bottom line, then it might not be worth doing, or it might need to be adjusted so that it does have an impact on revenue.

Given that raising money is one of the most important goals in philanthropy, ***the closer you can align yourself to the check, the more value you'll be perceived to have.*** This is why fundraisers get paid more money, because they are the ones closest to the check. Make sure that you are aligning yourself with the gifts that come in. Make sure that the degree of separation from your shop and the gifts is as little as possible. We are not the ones that are handed the checks, so our value can get lost in the background noise. However, our activity directly impacts the frequency and size of checks that an organization receives. We must make this visible to leadership.

We must track our impact on the bottom line. Remember that *what gets measured, gets managed.* If you implement a system in your shop to measure your impact on the bottom line and use the bottom-line litmus test to guide your projects, your impact on the bottom-line will increase. Your work will be more focused and your organization will raise more money. ***Your shop will be seen as a revenue generator rather than a cost center.*** You'll be viewed as an asset rather than a liability.

Focusing on the bottom line is something that fundraisers are forced to do because it's almost always tied directly to their goals. If it isn't, they are the closest to the check, so their value is usually pretty easy to determine from management's view. It's the most basic math, how many gifts did you solicit, how many said yes, and what was the total value for the year? Determining the actual fundraiser effort that went into each gift is another story and usually the check supersedes and outweighs the activity when determining the actual value of the fundraiser.

In a Prospect Development shop, there are so many activities that can be done and they all can be helpful, but some are more helpful than others and some can help to bring in more money than others. Given that

Prospect Development shops don't tend to have revenue goals, the activities that are in our goals or deemed important might not always be the most important. Therefore, it will require an additional effort on your part to make sure that your goals are in alignment with what has the highest ROI. This will require reflection on your activities. Think of the actual value of each activity. Trace the impact of each activity to actual gifts. Evaluate, rearrange, refocus and redirect your efforts so that they all impact revenue, so that you are expending the most effort on the activities with the highest value.

Fundraisers are like matchmakers. In one hand, they have a deck of cards that represents giving opportunities, and in the other they have a deck of cards that represents their prospects. Their job is to match the right gift opportunity with right prospect to maximize revenue and enhance the donor experience. Sometimes they build gift opportunities to match a prospect's capacity and inclination where one didn't previously exist. Prospect Development is responsible for building portfolios, determining a prospect's capacity, collecting data, and running analytics on interest and inclination.

If you focus your goals on uncovering viable prospects, ensure that their capacity is accurate, and that the data you have is actionable, then you will ensure that the right gift opportunity is matched with the right prospect at the highest-rate possible. If you are off on this, your fundraisers will be matching the wrong prospects with the wrong gift opportunities, thus either not asking enough or not presenting compelling enough cases to their prospects. Money will be left on the table and donor satisfaction levels will decrease. This can be the difference between your organization raising $100M a year instead of $300M a year. You can hire all the fundraisers in the world, but they are never going to bring you their full potential without a solid research shop.

The activities of a Prospect Development department allow for more revenue to be generated per fundraiser, and for more fundraisers to be hired to generate revenue. You have to talk to your managers about this. You have to set up systems to show your managers and senior leadership the value that you bring to the table in actual revenue. You have to think of Prospect Development in terms of dollars in the door. You want senior leadership to view Prospect Development as a revenue generator because we *are* a revenue generator. This is a different conversation that you have to have with your leadership and your management. It might feel awkward at first, but you must do it. You are not taking anything away from the fundraisers; you are not saying that you did their work. You are only saying to your manger, "This is the role that I played in landing that $50M gift, and I wanted to share this with you because my team is very excited to have played such an integral role in attaining this funding."

Keep it between you and senior leadership. This isn't something that needs to be said to the actual fundraisers, unless they initiate a conversation and thank you for your role in the gift. You don't want to become engaged in an ego battle on this. It isn't worth it. But don't let that stop you from showing the data to senior leadership, so that they can understand where gifts come from and the actual impact of cause and effect as it relates to the work that your department does. ***When senior leadership understands this, they will make sure that they are investing the organization's money wisely when hiring positions and setting compensation packages.***

If we don't show them this, how are they supposed to know? ***Our work is often buried beneath layers of the work of others.*** Senior leadership is not in the business of data forensics. Even if they have the ability to piece together history based on a data trail, they likely will not have the access or time to even run such an analysis on any particular gift let along all major, principal and transformative gifts. Understand this. ***It is up to us to ensure that our impact is visible to senior leadership and that we equip them with the data and analytics to empower them to ensure that they are running the most efficient organization and appropriately allocating resources to ensure the highest return on investment.***

Finding viable prospects is key. When I joined Stanford University's central office, the team was looking for a way to measure their impact on the bottom line. I began working on this problem immediately. I was able to put together a crude model based on historical data that measured giving patterns in prospects pre- and post-research rating and re-rating. The results were astonishing. Our prospecting and portfolio management activities translated into hundreds of millions of dollars per year in increased revenue. Our impact was astronomical. Totaled up over multiple years, it was over $1B. Make sure you are allocating enough resources into expanding your pipeline of viable, rated prospects. ***The more you add to the pipeline, the greater your impact on the bottom line.***

This is a new era, the era of big data. Seize this day. This is your key to the executive table. Identify as many viable prospects for every program as possible. Utilize data analytics to drive decision making, and unlock the giving potential of all prospects. Find out and record who they are, what they've done, what they are currently doing, what they are going to do in the future, and with whom all this happens. Right donor, right place, right time. Report this up to senior leadership so that they have a holistic view of the revenue causal chain. Empowered with this data, your leadership will make sure that your organization is harmonized.

Chapter 21

Our Value Proposition: How to Get Paid Like a Fundraiser

Do not simply tell me you are valuable. Demonstrate your true worth and you will be rewarded in accordance with your value.

When distilled down to their essence, all jobs in philanthropy share the same core principle: to add value. The form that value takes is what differs from job to job. Not every job in philanthropy is so inexorably tied to the gift that the value of that role can be easily thought of in terms of impact on the bottom line. The key is to understand the value that you bring to the table, and figure out how to quantify it in terms of dollars. What is the dollar value of the value of your work? How does the dollar value of your work translate to salary, resources, and budget?

Many, many years ago, I attend a conference presentation given by a VP of Advancement. Prior to this role as VP, the speaker had spent most of her career in Prospect Development. The talk was billed as an inspirational look into the potential career trajectory of someone from the world of Prospect Development into a senior leadership role. I was excited. This was the first time I had seen this career trajectory successfully happen for someone in our field. I thought ok, if it can happen for one of us, it can happen for all of us. Perhaps this will be the start of a new trend…

Unfortunately, the talk focused more on why researchers are not set up for success and why it is unlikely anyone in our field will ever follow this same path. The speaker even went so far as to say that if she ever had available funding for additional FTEs, she would always hire front line fundraisers and never researchers. In addition, she said that she didn't feel the need to increase researchers' salaries, because they were not flight risks and never came to her asking for higher salaries. She couldn't justify the value in ever adding a researcher over a fundraiser. She was under pressure to increase revenue, so naturally her focus tended to be on her front-line staff.

I left the presentation feeling deflated and confused. Could this be true? Is this the way that we are seen as a profession by our leadership? Is there something that happens, even to a researcher, when placed in a seat of responsibility for revenue that changes assumptions and strategy? While this was not what I was expecting to hear, and believe me, it took a while for me to get over the let-down, the speaker actually gave some very important data to those present that day: highly-critical feedback. Her talk was valuable in that it gave us a peek inside the mind of an executive. It allowed us to see ourselves from the vantage point of leadership, and to see what mattered to them and how our programs might not always be the most obviously aligned with the top priorities of our leadership.

My mind raced. I started to think about my job from a different vantage point. Prior to this moment I had been viewing my job through the lenses of a researcher and fundraiser but not that of senior leadership. It's not that I was oblivious to senior leadership and what they wanted but I hadn't experienced such a raw outpouring of the leadership point of view.

I began to rethink my approach to my work and asked myself and others a ton of questions such as:

- What if researchers were flight risks?
- What if we shopped around for jobs?
- What if we reinterpreted our work more in terms of partnership and relationships, and less on service?
- What if we focused our work more around actionable intelligence?
- What if we focused more on activities that increased the bottom line?
- What if we promoted ourselves and our work (respectfully, of course) so that our value became widely known by all in the office?
- What if we went to our managers after we had a direct impact on revenue in the millions of dollars and asked for an equity increase?
- What if we adopted these behaviors of fundraisers that served them well in terms of their bottom-line?

Most of the advice in this book not only serves the donors, the mission of our organizations, and our constituents, but it will also serve our profession and ourselves. It will ensure that we are assigned the appropriate place in the hierarchy of our office structure. With the appropriate placement, comes the ability to have maximum impact.

Let's look at our value proposition in very simple terms, translated to a mathematical equation:

(# of fundraiser's supported)

X (times)

(average percentage of revenue impact per fundraiser supported)

= value of data professional (as a multiple of 1 fundraiser)

Ideally, the average Researcher/Data Scientist should typically support anywhere between 5-15 front line fundraisers with the average being somewhere in the middle, around 9 (this is not to say that a 1/9 is ideal). In reality, this number can vary from 5 to somewhere in the upper 20s. This means that ***one researcher influences revenue generation as a multiple of themselves.***

That multiplier will depend on the number of front line fundraisers supported by each researcher and the percentage of revenue generation that you can link back to research per person. In my experience, the percentage of revenue generation can be anywhere from 20% to 1000%. So if you were to take the 9 fundraisers to every 1 researcher model and selected 33% as the percentage of revenue generation, then you would have a value proposition that equates the value of 1 researcher to that of the revenue generation of 3 total fundraisers. This is a low estimate. Try this exercise with your numbers.

If you were to translate the above example of a 9/1 ratio @ a 33% average share of revenue generation per fundraiser into our equation for determining value it would look like:

$$9 \times .33 = 3$$

(meaning your value is that of 3 fundraisers in terms of revenue generation)

9 *(# of fundraiser's supported)*

X (times)

.33 *(average percentage of revenue impact per fundraiser supported)*

= ***3*** *value of data professional (as a multiple of 1 fundraiser)*

Our reach is far. This is awesome news, right? Yet, when you look at pay disparity in our profession, you will almost always have to use a divider from the salary of one fundraiser to get to the salary of one data worker. Am I the only one this seems backwards to? If we are able to influence the revenue across 5-25 individuals, then our impact on the bottom line will always be far greater than one single fundraiser. If our impact is greater than one fundraiser, our salary should reflect that, right?

If our impact is so high, why are we paid so low? Simply put, we are not directly tied to the gifts. We are not the first degree from the gift. The further away you get from the gift, the harder it is to determine degree of impact. Since we are not fundraisers, we are not the ones who bring back the checks; ***we must get as close as possible to the act of getting the gift through ensuring that our actionable intelligence sparks gifts.***

If you send out actionable intelligence that results in the fundraiser taking an action that leads to the gift then you are two degrees away from the gift. That is about as close as we can get without being the actual solicitor. This kind of work receives recognition. The more you do the easier it is to showcase our true value.

We must align ourselves as closely as possible with our fundraisers and the gifts and practice bottom-line focused Precision Prospect Development. We must at all times be a constant reminder that we increase revenue per fundraiser and increase the number of fundraisers that can be hired. Make sure that you are tracking this, and can show how your work contributes to the growth in front-line fundraisers in your organization.

Examine your value proposition. Make sure that it is in alignment with what your organization values the most. You may have to adjust and or increase your value proposition if you are going to level up your pay scale. Be mindful of this as well. It might not just be all about the bottom-line for some of you.

What are other factors at play that are valued? Through analyzing your work through this lens of value, you can make the necessary adjustments to make sure that your value proposition is aligned with your organization's understanding of your value.

We tend to not do a very good job at expressing our value proposition. We tend to shy away from salary negotiations, from talking to leadership about our impact on gifts as they roll in. We tend to not always remain laser-focused on conducting our business with a bottom-lined focus. This does not serve us well. It might take some time to get used to viewing things in this way but the payoff is worth it. I am grateful that I attended that conference session and heard the words of that senior leader. If I hadn't, I might not have set off on this course in my career.

(*Note that this chapter is in no way meant to devalue the work of fundraisers. They have tough jobs and deserve to receive pay that is in accordance with their value. But this does not negate our right to be paid in accordance with our value. Through showing that our work impacts their success is in no way taking away credit from fundraisers for the work that they do. It is simply looking at a gift from a holistic perspective and understanding how they are generated. If we understand how gifts are generated then we can approach our business in a way to generates more.)

If you want to help our profession, yourself, and level the playing field when it comes to salary, you must pay attention to the following:

Value Proposition: If you want to increase your worth, increase your value proposition.

Shop Around: Don't be afraid to take that interview; don't be afraid to move to another organization.

Ask for an Increase: Don't be afraid to ask for a salary increase. Make sure to time it with a large, revenue-based success, like providing integral actionable intelligence for a large gift.

Track Your Impact on the Bottom-Line: Create a system and monitor your impact on the bottom-line. When a major gift comes in through the work of your team, make sure to let management know. You don't have to wave this flag in front of the fundraisers. However, when meeting with the Chief Development Officer, or the VP of Principal Gifts, or whomever you report to, make sure that you get this data into their hands so that they can have a true understanding of the real impact of your work in terms of dollars in the door.

Build Relationships: Build strong relationships with colleagues, especially the fundraisers you support. Allocating time for this as bonding with your stakeholders is of equal or more value than providing high quality deliverables.

Find Prospects: The more prospects you add to the pipeline, the greater your impact on the bottom line. This is the foundation of our revenue generation.

Practice *Precision Prospect Development*: Increase actionable intelligence, practice bottom-line research, think like a fundraiser, plug into the DNA of your organization.

Chapter 22

ADD VALUE

The essence of all of our job functions is simple: add value.

The value of the work of Prospect Development can be hard to determine if we don't do a good job of tracking and measuring impact. It was argued earlier in this book that Prospect Development is a revenue generator. Since we are not directly tied to the gifts, it can be hard to come up with an actual value for our work if we do not take the initiative and begin to implement systems that can translate all that we do in terms of actual value.

The core essence of all of our jobs is to add value. Value comes in many forms. Translating it into financial terms is important for your bottom line, and should be something we can all accomplish if we put our minds to it. ***To increase your worth, increase your value proposition.***

What does your organization value the most? As you take the necessary steps to get plugged into your organization's DNA, think about, and gather data, around what your organization values. What does leadership, your manager, and your constituents value the most? Ask them. Be up front and honest. Then reassess your work to make sure that you are conducting your business in a way that is hyper-focused on these values.

What is rewarded is what is valued. As you look into what your organization values, also look into what types of activities or outcomes or behaviors that your organization rewards. You might not learn everything when you ask what is valued. Sometimes what is valued is not necessarily what is rewarded. It is important to take this extra step and combine your data on what is valued with what is rewarded in order to get a more precise picture of what your organizations values.

What are the goals for your organization, your fundraisers? ***Understanding the goals will help you to have a better understanding of what is valued.*** Goals will tell you what is temporarily valued on an annual basis. Incorporate into your annual planning, meetings with fundraisers, and each department that you work with to walk through their goals. Make sure that your goals are aligned and are in support of their goals.

Opportunities for adding value abound. We are constantly encountering them in almost everything we experience. The problem is that we don't always recognize them. Or, if we do recognize them, we might not know what the *next best action* to take is in order to maximize value. Utilize the data you collect on what is valued and rewarded to recognize the best opportunities for adding value, and marry that with the best action. As you work with each unit across your organization, attend strategy meetings, and meet with constituents, make sure that you are incorporating this data into your interactions so that you can have the greatest impact. Make sure that you seize these opportunities and add value each and every time you are able to. Seek out additional areas for opportunity to add value.

If you are unclear on what your organization values or rewards, you can always start with the top assets at your organization. As stated in Chapter 14, "Data as an Asset", the top assets at most philanthropic organizations can be filed into five buckets: people/talent, endowment/finances, data, mission, and brand. Think of how your work has an impact in each of these areas. How does what you do add to the value of your organization's assets? Is there any work that you do that has no impact on any of these assets? How much of your time and effort is spent in adding value to any given area? ***Are your time and energy proportionally-allocated properly to the appropriate value?*** Make adjustments to ensure that it is. Don't spend time working on projects that have little to no value.

The more we know about what our organizations value and reward, the more value we are able to deliver. Take the time to distill all of your work and activity through your organization's value filter. Make sure that the activities and work of your department are aligned as closely as possible to your organization's values. ***The more value you add, the more you will be valued.***

Chapter 23

VALUE EVERYTHING

Everything you do has a value. Determining the actual value of each thing is vital to be able to precisely proportion the appropriate amount of energy to be allocated to each thing.

If you were given ten tasks to complete, all of equal difficulty, all requiring the same use of resources, but only had time to complete five with no idea of the true net value for completing each action, or the exponential future value of completing each action, how would you select the five tasks to complete? You could use your intuition, use your best educated guess, your gut feeling, randomly pick five…but you would never know if you picked the right five in terms of value.

One way to solve this problem is to assign values to as many activities within your shop as you can think of. Start small. There is no need to value everything all at once. Begin valuing each thing you do, and eventually you will build out a portfolio of valuations. For example, what is the actual value of a research rating, of employment information, of education information, of an email address? What is the value of a particular record, or a phone call, or an event, or a prospect visit, dinner, or meeting? What is the value of someone's current business title and company information, their education, their twitter handle, their LinkedIn page? Balance this out with a determination of the cost of each activity.

If you are able to determine the value of some of your key activities, you can then know where to spend your time; if you know this, then you can spend your time wisely, make informed decisions, drive for greatest impact, and bring in maximum dollars in the door. You will understand your cost/value ratio and be able to direct your resources for maximum ROI.

Chapter 24

SUPERIOR SERVICE

"I've learned that people will forget what you said, people will forget what you did, but people will never forget how you made them feel."

Maya Angelou

Prospect Development is traditionally thought of as being in the service business. We provide many services throughout an organization. I will not argue this. However, I will argue that by being in the service business, ***we are actually in the relationship business.*** We are actually just like fundraisers in that regard. They are in the relationship business with donors and provide them with a service; we are in a relationship business with our constituents and provide them with a service. ***The core essence of our service is actually very simple. It is connection.***

As human beings we all seek connectedness. We are social creatures. When someone reaches out to you with a service request, they are making a connection. ***How you handle that connection will determine the direction and frequency of all future connections.*** Are you currently conducting yourself in a manner that is creating and cultivating positive, productive connections? Do you care about the success of your constituents? Do you approach their problems with compassion or judgement? Are you setting a tone of collaboration?

The above quote from Maya Angelou is one of the guiding principles I have always used to run my shops. As providers of services, the relationships we build will greatly affect our impact. The more we are able to successfully partner with our constituents, the higher our percentage of successful projects, and more action will be taken from our actionable intelligence; the greater our impact, the better the donor experience, the greater that success will be achieved on all levels.

There is a ripple effect here. It all begins with your first encounter with a stakeholder. Make sure you are responsive, friendly, positive, and relatable. Spend time and effort on cultivating authentic connections. Make sure that you address and take care of their needs. Make sure that you are viewed as a valuable contributor and not a roadblock.

If you don't cultivate connections and create a collaborative working partnership with your stakeholders, you essentially relegate yourself and your team to be order-takers. Many Prospect Development departments operate as order-takers and not as partners. Sometimes this is a conscious choice, sometimes this is the result of a lack of the cultivation of connections. Because if you don't cultivate connections, you are essentially an order-taker.

We want to be partners, influencers, the drivers of change. We want to have an impact. We want our efforts to bear fruit. We want to make it rain. We want our constituents to succeed. The only way to achieve this at maximum level is through consciously cultivating positive, authentic connections with everyone in our office that we encounter.

I have worked alongside many different researchers and noticed time and again that ***the most successful were those who focused on cultivating connections***. Even if they lacked technical expertise and/or their work was sub-par, their connectedness resulted in higher performing actionable intelligence over and above the technical experts who neglected to cultivate connection.

If you are able to cultivate positive, collaborative relationships with your stakeholders, the sky is the limit. You will cease to exist at the end of a dead-end street, receiving orders via a queue. You will become an active partner. You will learn more about who your constituents are and what makes them tick. The more you learn about who they are, the better you'll be able to hone in on exactly what they want, and be able to deliver that to them. You'll learn how to speak their language, which will open up a vast array of new opportunities for engagement and deliverables. You'll build rapport and through this, you can push them in a positive way. You'll gain access to what they are working on at a level you had never before imagined. You'll learn their goals, and know what they need to achieve and when they need to achieve it.

With this knowledge you can deliver the most precise, actionable intelligence possible. You can take things so much further. Once you learn what they need to accomplish in order to be successful, you can make sure that your work is aligned with their end goals. The more your work contributes to their success, the more indispensable you'll become. The bonds will continue to strengthen on multiple levels.

Another side benefit from creating a strong working relationship, is that they will be more charitable with your work. They will not look for errors. They will be quick to forgive, and less likely to critique. Add this to everything else and you can then begin to feel empowered to take more and more calculated risks without fear of reprisal. This will provide a level of safety that will allow you to experiment, get creative, and push the envelope. The fear of error removed will actually allow you to move faster and with more precision. It will decrease your error rate, requiring less time proofing and/or worrying about potential errors. You can collaborate more with your constituents on pushing the envelope. You will achieve far greater results with less effort and have fun all the while. Your job satisfaction will improve, and your stress will decrease.

Make sure that you and your team are following-up with your constituents periodically and have regular check-ins so that you can make sure that they feel like they are on track for success and that their needs are being met by you and your department. This only takes a few minutes of your time, and the ROI is huge here. This added layer of concierge-style service goes such a long way. My research team spends a few minutes chatting with their fundraiser partners about a majority of their research requests so that they can make sure that they are delivering exactly what is needed. This dialogue-style method saves the researchers time, allows them to gauge the importance of the request and to determine how much time to spend on the request. It strengthens the bond between researcher and fundraiser, and allows for some extra information to be exchanged and figured out so that the end result is more precisely on the mark.

My analyst team periodically goes out and touches base with constituents on their dashboards and makes sure that they are getting the most value out of them. This 15-minute conversation results in more satisfied end users, higher usage rates, higher ROIs for our dashboards, and stronger bonds between my analysts and their constituents that sets the stage for even better dashboards. Again, it is all about cultivating connection. It is hard to do that if you solely allow a queue to manage your relationships.

Another aspect of superior service is making sure to take care of your constituents and have them leaving your presence feeling like you've done justice by them. To do this, you actually have to care about them and their success. When someone comes to you and has a question that doesn't fall within your realm, don't just send them away with a no. Make sure to connect them with the person that either has the answer or is most likely to have the answer. Take pride in your work. Don't just point them there, make the introduction. Follow-up. Exert that bit of extra energy to close the loop and take care of your colleagues. If you do know the answer, but it doesn't fall within your core function, answer the question, but afterwards make sure to follow-up with the person whose core function it falls under so that they are aware that one of their constituents had that question.

This knowledge can help inform the relationship with their constituents, and might spark additional action to ensure that their constituent is equipped with the knowledge they need to perform their function.

One of the core values at City of Hope is compassion. I find that it is hard to do the job of Prospect Development successfully without operating from a place of compassion. We can't judge our constituents if they don't understand data. That would be poor service. If they don't understand, it is our job to provide a level of service that allows them to get to a place of at least being able to functionally operate with data. Through cultivating relationships on the foundation of compassion you will never reach a roadblock that you cannot overcome.

Cultivating positive connections will help to set the tone of your department, and will create a positive, collaborative, trusting culture. Your department can really set the tone for how the entire office works together because of the amount of people we work with. Be acutely aware of how you are interacting with colleagues and the example that you are setting.

Take care of your constituents, and build solid partnerships in the process. Make sure that you are never turning anyone away feeling bad about their experience with you or your team. Spend that extra few minutes whenever and wherever possible to add that additional layer of a personal touch. Let compassion drive your encounters. Set your sights on providing deliverables that are as closely aligned with their goals as possible. The more your work adds to their success, the more successful you will be.

Chapter 25

THE KEY TO BUILDING SOLID RELATIONSHIPS

Forge yourself into a skeleton key that can open up even the coldest of hearts.

Prospect Development is in the relationship business. We are connection cultivators. Our success hinges just as much on how good we are at engaging with our constituents as it does on our technical expertise. Building and maintaining, solid, meaningful relationships takes time. It can also take practice. Make sure that you are allocating time to build relationships with your constituents.

This will require that you put yourself out there. Invite folks out to lunch; begin each meeting with a few minutes of small talk. Bond over shared interests. Throughout the process, remain true to yourself and your style. Make sure that you are operating from a place of authenticity. This won't work if you go about building your relationships as a chore or as a means to an end. Don't collect relationships because you know that they are valuable. You have to have a certain level of care and compassion for your constituents embedded in your core. This is the key to building solid relationships.

You have to genuinely want your constituents to be successful. You have to genuinely want to help them to operationalize and streamline their business processes. You have to want to deliver data that will drive their success. You have to want them to enjoy working with you and you have to want to enjoy working with them. Energy transmits from one entity to another; if you carry yourself with an energy of acceptance, care and compassion, you will draw in your constituents like a magnet. They will know that you are there to help and will welcome you with open arms. You will build solid relationships. If you are charitable with your constituents, they will be charitable with you.

There may be times when you have to remind your constituents that you are there for them. Don't forget to invest in this kind of relationship reassurance. I find that I am constantly reminding my constituents that I am there for them and that they can count on me to have their back. This is almost always met by appreciation and a reciprocal of reassurance that they too are appreciative of the relationship and that they are also here for me. This helps to keep the relationship open and free so that the lines of communication remain strong and when a hiccup occurs you are able to nip it in the bud quickly and get back on track.

It also helps to prevent any potential office gossips from wreaking havoc on your relationships and career through the spread of falsehood. I am constantly baffled as to why people spread falsehood around offices attempting to create discord. When you have a solid bond with someone, they are less likely to take the bait of a gossip and rely on their actual experience with you to inform them of who you are as a person.

(On a side note, don't be that person who says bad things about other people. There is almost never a time where this is appropriate. It will never serve your relationships. Be very careful when folks approach you with this kind of behavior. They are almost always doing so with some sort of selfish motivation. Although it may come across as insight or inside information, be careful and put the validity of this kind of data low on your scale of reliability and allow your personal experience to be the true guide. Gossip is bad for business and just plain bad all around. I try to follow the advice that if I don't have something nice to say about someone I don't say anything at all. I am constantly puzzled as to how people are so quick to believe negative things about individuals that they have never even met when one person reports back that they are "difficult" or "hard to get along with" or "not very good at their jobs" etc. the list goes on and on. Why would you give your power over to someone in this situation and potentially rob yourself of having an amazing new bond by trusting this faulty data?

I've experienced this same situation over and over again where there are colleagues in the office who move in quick on new employees, try to befriend them, take them out to lunch and give them the "411" on people they don't like in order to taint their view so as to get more people to have the same dysfunctions that they have thus minimizing the fact that they are operating in a dysfunctional manner and causing problems. If they can "convert" more people to have dysfunctional relationships with the same people as them then they can hide their accountability with management and use the power of numbers to defend themselves in the face of problems that they are causing and shift accountability to an unwitting colleague. Don't be toxic like this and don't tolerate this from your colleagues or employees. It is a shame that humans have not evolved beyond this kind of behavior and it saddens my heart when I witness it or see the negative impact and consequences it can have on someone's life.

Arm yourself against giving up your power to gossips and proceed with caution when receiving this kind of information. Set a tone where this is not acceptable. Let personal experience be your guide. Be careful when you are interacting with someone who operates in this fashion as they are likely toxic and will only bring trouble. In the words of Gandalf in *Lord of the Rings, Fellowship of the Ring,* "Do not be too eager to deal out… judgement. For even the wise cannot see all ends.")

This is not to say that you have to have a solid bond with every one of your constituents. You will definitely forge stronger bonds with some more than others. There may always be a few that you can't reach or who can't reach you. Allow for this to happen, but don't allow for the lack of a strong connection to deteriorate your ability to care for their success. In the instances where connection does not come as naturally or as easily, it will require you to become somewhat detached from the relationship. Meaning, don't allow yourself to become upset or bothered if you have constituents who do not play nice or who do not seem to have your best interests at heart. Understand where they are coming from and protect yourself from their negativity, not by throwing negativity back, but by continuing to showcase compassion. Continue to look for that right balance or combination to unlock the most productive, positive relationship possible.

An analogy I use with my team for relationship building is that of a key or a combination to a lock. We all have the potential to relate with everyone we come across given that we are all undergoing the human experience. We have a relationship building algorithm that we utilize when we socialize. Constantly refine this so that you are able to build solid relationships. It simply requires finding the right combination that you can use like a key.

We are all made up of data. We are the combination of our individual chemical makeup, combined with the data of our life experiences, filtered through a chemical reaction with the data of the world around us. How we relate to each person is built upon a unique combination of the coming together of what we choose to share or display from our unique datasets, and how that data is interpreted. We have unlimited data within us we can pull from in order to cultivate a connection. As you engage with your constituents, be open with them, and see if you can use your relationship building algorithm to find the right data key so that they will open up to you. As they open up to you, continue to utilize your key to forge a solid connection. The more you practice, the better you will get, and the more you will forge yourself into a skeleton key that can warm up even the coldest of hearts.

Chapter 26

BUILDING YOUR BRAND

"Perception is reality."

Lee Atwater

A long time ago, I used to watch the HBO series *Entourage*. I will never forget this one episode where the main character, Vince, who is a famous, up and coming Hollywood actor, is shopping around for a new talent agency to represent him. He goes to a handful of meetings and gets practically the same pitch from each agency. They all run through a PowerPoint slideshow of big brands like Apple and Coke, ending with a slide with Vince's picture and tell him that he is a brand just like these companies, and that they are going to make his brand just as loved around the world as the blue chip companies.

Whether we like it or not, we can't stop the fact that we ourselves are all brands, so to speak. "Perception is reality." We are constantly being judged by everyone we encounter. How we carry ourselves, how we interact with colleagues, what we wear, how we talk, how we show up in meetings, how we collaborate, all go into crafting our own, personal brand. The value of our personal brand is thus always changing, and is either becoming more or less valuable with each step we take forward in time.

This all goes into how others perceive us. **How others perceive us will drive how they interact with us.** If your constituents perceive you as approachable, fun and helpful, they are so much more likely to engage with you, to let you into their world, to open up to you on a level that will maximize your working relationship.

We are service providers. As service providers, relationships are of vital importance. In the chapter on *Superior Service,* I argued that we are not really in the service business, but in the relationship business, and the relationship business is all about connection. Connection is driven by perception. How are you being perceived? Does it align with how you think you should be perceived? Does it match how you want to be perceived? Does it cultivate meaningful connection?

What do you want your personal brand to represent? Are you currently operating in a way that supports your vision for your personal brand? What changes do you need to make to get your behavior in alignment with your vision for yourself? How is your personal brand currently being perceived? Do the perceptions match yours? If not, how can you change this? When your constituents think of you, do they smile, or does their stomach drop?

You must invest in cultivating your personal brand. It can be the difference between success and failure. You must invest time and effort into aligning your behaviors, actions, and appearance with your vision and goals for yourself. If you are not investing in your brand and not achieving the results you desire, then you may want to start here. You likely need to invest in yourself and your brand.

Building a brand requires marketing and relationship building. You have to market yourself in the way that you want to be perceived. You have to make sure that your brand matches your vision. This will require you to put yourself out there and that is ok. If you prefer to sit on the sidelines and prefer receiving requests through the queue and don't want to attend meetings then you don't have to worry as much about your personal brand because it will most likely match your desire of being alone. But if you want a seat at the table, if you want to increase your influence, if you want to achieve maximum impact from your work, then it will require you to put yourself out there and to create a brand for yourself that is personable, fun, creative, smart, focused, and talented.

There are a lot of books out there on building your brand, and I would suggest if this is an area where you find you need some work, you might want to look into reading one of them. This chapter is just meant to shine light on this area and to make sure that we data folks are aware that the perceptions of others are powerful and are a determining factor in our career trajectory. Make sure that as you build your brand you are staying authentic to yourself, not forcing things, overcompensating, or coming off as unnatural. Make sure that your brand-building strategies are ones that add value to your brand.

Chapter 27

Decision Tree: Matching Resources to Prospects for Increased Engagement and Revenue Generation

The following chapter outlines an exercise that will allow you to collect the data necessary to build out the first layer of The Platform.

Have you or your fundraisers ever taken stock of all of the resources that you have available to uncover prospects and move them through the solicitation cycle? Do your fundraisers know who and what they have at their disposal to engage their portfolio and raise gifts? Do they know where they fall short or where they have strengths? The following exercise is one of the most valuable that you can go through with your fundraisers. The outcome will be the creation of a decision tree matrix that matches resources with prospects to unlock more relationships and gifts. The outcome will form the foundation of *The Platform.*

After you have gone through the exercise, you can take the results and create a matrix that will help all fundraisers to intimately know every tool they have available to aid them in fundraising. You can provide them with a way to plug in their prospects and determine what their *next best action* should be for engagement and solicitation. You can build some algorithms so help automate as much of the process as possible and to apply it en masse at scale.

How you answer these questions will be determined by your unique organization and what you have available at your disposal. You may find that through doing this exercise there are areas of weakness that need to be strategically worked on and built out.

Decision Tree Exercise:

1. What are your potential resources that you can use to move prospects through the solicitation cycle? Who can help? What can help?

    Examples of Who can help:

    - Board Members
    - Volunteers
    - Donors
    - Faculty
    - Staff
    - Employees
    - Your Network
    - Colleagues/Other Fundraisers
    - Prospect Development

    Examples of what can help:

    - Database
    - Phone
    - Internet
    - Email
    - Periodicals
    - Vendor

2. What are your possible outreach methods? What are your *next best actions*?

Examples of potential outreach methods:

- Invite to Event
- Invite to Small Dinner
- Invite to Tour
- Email
- Letter
- Phone
- In-Person encounter
- Survey
- Peer Screening

Actions can be performed by:

- You
- Someone from another department (too many to list out here)

3. What are the key data elements that you can use to match your resources to your prospects?

    Examples (Not meant to be an exhaustive list, make sure to include information from both spouses for all fields):

    - Research Rating
    - Job Title
    - Company
    - Industry
    - Past Employment
    - For-Profit Board Memberships
    - Non-Profit Board Memberships
    - Alma Mater
    - Degree
    - Degree Year
    - Interests
    - Children
    - Children School
    - Relationships
    - Analytics
    - Last Gift Date
    - Last Gift Amount
    - Last Gift Fund
    - Lifetime Giving
    - # of Gifts
    - First Gift Date
    - Gifts to Other Organizations
    - Other Data Elements that Link to Your Organization

4. What are the key data elements that can help to determine *next best action*?

Examples (Not meant to be exhaustive):

- Research Rating
- Job Title
- Company
- Industry
- Past Employment
- For-Profit Board Memberships
- Non-Profit Board Memberships
- Alma Mater
- Degree
- Degree Year
- Interests
- Children
- Children School
- Relationships
- Analytics
- Last Gift Date
- Last Gift Amount
- Last Gift Fund
- Lifetime Giving
- # of Gifts
- First Gift Date
- Gifts to Other Organizations
- Other Data Elements that Link to Your Organization

5. What are the various programs and/or gift opportunities and/or volunteer opportunities you have available?

Department Examples	**Gift Examples**	**Volunteer Examples**
Annual Giving	Recurring Gift	Peer Screening
Planned Giving	Estate Gift	Event Host
Corporate Giving	Gift in Kind	Museum Docent
Foundation Giving	Grant	Hospital Greeter
Major Giving	Gift of Securities	Volunteer Solicitor
Principal Giving	Named Gift	Board Member
Stewardship		Committee Member

After you have conducted this exercise, you will have the foundational elements for your platform. You will have the raw data that can inform your options for *next best action*s in any possible situation. You will have all of the raw data necessary to explore potential donor pathways.

(*NOTE that this chapter is not meant to be a comprehensive outline for how to build a platform, but to give the basic introduction on how to collect the right data to begin building your own platform. Integrate this into your workflow, and take it as far as you can.)

Chapter 28

THE SIX KEY ELEMENTS OF PRECISION

The Who *refers to the people involved in the communication or activity.*
The What *refers to the actual content of the communication or activity.*
The When *refers to the timing of the communication or activity.*
The Where *refers to location of the communication or activity.*
The Why *refers to purpose of the communication or activity.*
The How *refers to the way in which content is communicated or acted upon.*

You probably remember this lesson from elementary school. ***All activity and interpersonal communication is comprised of a blend of the who, the what, the when, the where, the why and the how.*** We must become masters of the interplay of these *six variables* in order to master the art of *Precision Prospect Development* and ensure our work is precisely honed in on and aligned with our organization's DNA. ***Success depends on how masterfully and precisely you can align your activities with these variables in any given situation.*** This is all about precision.

These are the six key elements to consider when taking any and every action. You must understand these six key elements and how they are represented and reflected in each and every aspect of your office and life in general. These *six elements* are the underlying building blocks of your organization's (collective ecosystem's) DNA. Every moving piece of your organization has multiple factors, all uniquely made up of their own variables of the *six elements.* ***How you get in alignment with your organization's DNA is simply a weaving of your six elements with the six elements that you are faced with at any given moment.*** You must become a master data-blender of these elements in order to achieve success. You must master the precision of this with the steady hand of a surgeon.

Pay attention to each one of these variables with everything you do. This is vital to maximizing impact. Think about all of your activities and run them through these *six variables* and ask, with each variable, if you are positioning in the appropriate way to achieve your intended goal.

Some examples you can ask yourself are:

Who are the influencers at my organization? What does leadership value the most? What does my manager value the most?

What are the goals of my constituents? When is the best time to approach a given constituent with a new discovery? When is the best time to interact with my constituents?

How am I coming across with my communication style? Is now the right time to tell my constituent that we were not able to find a solution to their problem?

What am I trying to achieve? Are the people I am copying on this email the right people? Am I including too many or too few? Did I invite the right people to this meeting? Did I include the right people on this project?

Is now the right time to embark on this project? Is now the right time to ask for a raise? Is this the right space to work on this project? Is this the right place to hold this retreat? Why am I doing this project?

Have you ever put a lot of care and work into a project only to see it not go anywhere? Later on you might even see someone do something almost identical, yet they are able to achieve success. This is likely because of the interplay of the *six elements*. ***Slight variations in any of the six elements can mean the difference between success and failure. This is why precision is so important.*** It's like in *Star Wars* when Luke had one shot to fire torpedoes through the tiny hole in the *Death Star*. If his shot was even slightly off, it wouldn't go through. Sometimes our success hinges on something so small, that even the tiniest variation in the wrong direction can be the downfall of something potentially great. If we trust in ourselves and walk the path of precision we will lessen the chance that pivotal opportunities will pass us by.

Many years ago, my team was given a rather large and challenging project of creating a data driven culture. This included creating and implementing a prospect management system, building dashboards to reflect fundraiser activity, and building training materials and training folks in how to use all of the new systems. This was no small undertaking. We had less than a year to implement, and had to have results that could be presented to our board of directors in a tight timeframe. This project required a ton of work and had a lot of different moving pieces. At one point, after we were initially seeing success with the deployment of our new prospect management systems, a colleague from another team said to me, "This is going to fail, you know that, right?" I was confused. This came from one of my IT data partners. He was on a different team that didn't report up through me, but he was nevertheless a total data person, in a position of supporting these new systems.

I replied back, "The usage data is showing this is going to succeed. Am I missing something? What makes you think this is going to fail?"

He said, "I've tried this exact same thing a couple of times over the last 15 years, and it always ends up in failure. So this, too, will end up in failure."

I replied, "It can't possibly be the same because the conditions are not the same as they are now. How you went about doing the project was completely different. The team is not the same, there are more people open to operating this way now that there were then. The timing is completely different. We have a board goal that is motivating leadership to back this in a way that they were not able to back it before. This change in leadership direction is creating an environment that is increasing participation. This project probably couldn't have been successful then, no matter how hard you tried, because the organization simply wasn't ready for it yet."

I don't think I was able to convince him, but it was clear to me that there were vast differences in the *six elements* in all of these situations. The way I went about the project, versus the way he went about the project were under completely different circumstances. The way I weaved my elemental approach with the DNA of the organization at the time helped to ensure and solidify success. The project ended up succeeding. He was the only one who was not fully on board whereas in the previous iteration many years ago he would have been my biggest ally. In the case of this similar project many years later, he was a roadblock. It was unfortunate because I think his past self would have been super excited by our progress and he robbed himself of the joy of finally getting this project pushed through.

Don't allow yourself to be robbed of success because you are trapped in the past by an incomplete understanding of the *six elements* at your organization and how they work and how you can utilize them to invigorate your work with a precision method that increases your success rate and removes your attachment to negative outcomes from previous attempts.

Chapter 29

THE HOW VS. THE WHAT

How you deliver content not only alters perceptions, but also alters content.

Did you know that how you deliver content can actually alter the meaning of that content? This is something I call ***the how factor***. Because of *the how factor*, ***how you deliver content is actually more important than the content of what you are delivering.*** Too often we get caught up in the raw data or basic content and think that if only we stick to the facts and present the data, the data will speak for itself and whatever action that needs to be taken will be taken by those who are exposed to the data.

I don't think I've ever witnessed this happen successfully. I've noticed repeatedly that *how* I go about communicating the results of a project is so much more important than *what* I said. One of the key ingredients to success is how you deliver your work, how you communicate with others.

How. We spend so much time executing our work, building products, creating business processes, writing research profiles, and running analysis that it is important to spend enough time developing and implementing a strategy of how to take that work and make sure that it is presented in such a way as to have maximum impact and not get brushed aside.

Tesla was one of the greatest minds that ever lived and was filled with brilliant inventions and ideas yet we are only benefitting from a small fraction of what he was capable of because he had a hard time with implementing a successful *how* strategy. Time and again his brilliance was not allowed to thrive because of the circumstances in which he found himself due to his inability to master with precision how to go about ensuring success. This same pattern has repeated itself throughout history countless of times and is currently happening to in multiple places on the planet as you read these pages.

Mastering *the how factor* requires some salesmanship. I don't want to boil this down or oversimplify this concept to salesmanship, but a great deal of how to master *the how factor* intersects with salesmanship. As you work on how you come across and how you interact with folks and develop strategies around how to go about achieving success, think of how is the best way to win someone over to your idea or to your project. Sometimes that way of looking at the problem can help to solve it.

It is important that you get away from your desk and develop relationships with your key stakeholders so that you can best learn how to ensure success. If you don't know the ins and outs of their style, flow, or pet peeves, you will not be able to deliver information in a way that is precisely-tuned for maximum absorption. For example, if you have a message to give to the Senior VP but don't have enough data on them to know how to deliver the message, you are in danger of delivering in a way that will not get through, whereas a minor tweak may change their perception from negative to positive.

How are you delivering your work to your constituents?

Is your current delivery method the most effective?

Does your interaction with your constituents draw them in or push them away?

Think about your how factor. Make sure that you are in tune with your constituents, and are interacting with them in a way that they can relate to. Make sure that how you go about things is going to deliver success with all that you do. Don't let a faulty or unrefined delivery method prevent viable projects from being implemented. Set your how factor algorithm to collect data from your environment so that you are equipped with the tools to deploy custom delivery methods for each and every person and situation.

Chapter 30

THE WHEN: TIMING

"There is timing in everything. Timing in strategy cannot be mastered without a great deal of practice."

Miyamoto Musashi

Is this the right time? If not now, when would be the best time? Ask yourself these two questions with all that you do. ***The timing of when we deliver our projects can be the difference between success and failure.*** If the timing is off, your audience might not even be aware of what it is that you are presenting. It might not even register to them, and thus because it doesn't register, they won't remember it when the proper time comes to implement the idea or project.

Mastering the art of timing often requires discipline, patience, presence, confidence and restraint. Have you ever had a really cool project idea or insight or dashboard that you were so excited about and you couldn't wait to share it with your supervisor? You bring it to your 1:1 and have it in your pile of things to discuss. The entire meeting, you're waiting to be able to pull out this project and get feedback. You can feel your excitement. However, you notice that something is a little off. Your manager seems to be preoccupied with other matters and is a little frazzled. You want to share your insight but you are not sure if this is the right time. Your manager informs you that the board wants a certain report and they want it by tomorrow. This is all your manager wants to talk about. But you have this awesome thing you just can't wait to share.

What do you do? Is now the right time to share your new idea? Do you think your manager will be able to focus and understand the magnitude of your idea? Probably not. Even though you have this excitement built up, it is best to hold off and wait a few more days when your manager is in a space to absorb and understand your new idea. It might feel like an eternity to wait, but if you don't wait, you will likely encounter disappointment if you try to force it in the current situation which is not conducive to success.

I have been in this situation countless times. The times that I didn't have the discipline to wait, the project was ignored and didn't gain traction. I didn't receive much from my manager in terms of a positive response. I would walk away disappointed and feel unheard. I didn't like how this felt.

Through trial and error, I learned how important timing is as an ingredient for success. I became better at learning when was the right time to share certain information so that it is given the proper attention and the proper decision can be made or the proper feedback can be given. Learning this also allowed me to have a better relationship with my supervisors because I knew how to navigate our relationship better and operate in a way that was more supportive of both of us and our shared success.

Don't be afraid to sit on something and wait for the window of opportunity to open up. This requires discipline. My team always has a running list of projects that would be great to implement, but timing has prevented us from moving forward. We keep track of them, and as soon as the timing is right, we activate them. Whenever we come up with an idea or dream up a project that seems like it would be a big value add, we always ask, "Is this the right time?" If it is, we implement. If it isn't, we put it on hold, and monitor the atmosphere for the proper conditions to implement. When the proper conditions are on the horizon, we implement. The speed with which we are able to implement and meet the timing is often greeted by enthusiasm and amazement by our constituents.

Sometimes we would do our best to plant seeds for projects to speed up the timing so that folks are ready for it faster. This can be accomplished by steering the *six elements* so that they open up a window of timing sooner than it normally would have been open if you hadn't worked with *six elements* with precision. In order to do this, you must do your best to be present and live in that moment to fully understand the cause and effect happening around you.

The window is a good analogy for timing. Windows of opportunity abound. They are constantly opening and closing all around us, everywhere we go. They represent potentialities that could be birthed from the raw materials of existence. As you plug into the DNA of your surroundings, pay close attention to the windows of opportunity that align with your vision and goals and those of the organization. Look at what causes windows to open and close. Tune into this and you can initiate the circumstances for opportunities to open up.

Being conscious of timing doesn't mean you have to always wait and take a back-seat approach. Adjusting your timing algorithm to be in tune with your surroundings will ensure that you are speeding things up and slowing things down and taking the appropriate action at the right time in order to move things forward. This includes doing things that push boundaries in order to adjust timing.

Chapter 31

PLUG INTO YOUR ORGANIZATION'S DNA

"The natural laws of the universe are so precise that we don't even have any difficulty building spaceships that send people to the moon and we can time the landing with the precision of a fraction of a second."

Bob Proctor, Philosopher

As stated in one of the opening chapters of this book, each nonprofit organization is a living, collective organism made up of a multitude of moving parts: employees, donors, volunteers, technology, finances, departments, world events, leadership, goals, mission, and more. Each of these moving parts is made up of a unique combination of variables representing the *six elements.* As a living organism, our organizations have an underlying DNA code that is at the core foundation of its structure. Because our organizations are living, organic, collective entities, what works at one organization will not necessarily work at another. What works at one organization might need modifications in order to work at another. What works for one organization might work at another a year out in the future. One size does not fit all when it comes to developing your Prospect Development program and implementing strategies. How do you know what is going to work best at your organization, at what level, and at what time? How can you fine tune your work, your department, and your flow to match that of your organization?

In order to get in alignment with your organization and maximize your impact and success, you must plug into your organization's essence. You must plug into your organization's DNA. One of the best ways to achieve success through practicing *Precision Prospect Development* is through plugging into the DNA of your organization at every level, from micro to macro, from individual to department to enterprise. This is the only way to sync all activities so as to operate in a seamless fashion that will best meet the needs of your organization, further your organization's mission, and optimize the donor experience. You have to custom-tailor all of your business processes so that they seamlessly fit your organization to a T.

What does it mean to be plugged into your organization's DNA? To plug into your organization's DNA means to become acutely aware of as much of the goings on as possible: the goals, the strategies, the mission, the employees, the departments, the business processes, the progress, the data, and the prospects. For example, to be plugged into the DNA of the staff is to know what they are capable of undertaking at any given moment, and what they are in need of most at any given moment to push them across the finish line of success. In order to do this you must put yourself out there and you must collect as much data about your organization as you can. This is the only way to master the art of syncing all of your activities so that they are always occurring at the right time and including the right people.

When you are intimately tied to the DNA of your organization you will notice things that need attention. You will notice what needs more attention than others and you'll be able to determine the urgency of the need. Our job is about solving business challenges and finding solutions and solutioning for needs. As you look out in the collective organization your algorithms will pick up patterns and those patterns will provide you with guidance on what to do. Listen closely and you will see.

How do you get plugged into your organization's DNA? The formula is simple: ***Observe. Analyze. Get in sync. Implement with precision.***

How do you know in what direction things are headed? Start by taking a step back and being an observer and gather data. Understand as much as you can about the *six elements* that make up the foundation of each and everything you encounter. Once you have gathered your data, you then have to analyze it. Your analysis will form the strategies on how to best precision- align yourself in every situation. In other words, it will allow you to get in sync with what you discover. Follow the advice as outlined in this book. Most chapters in this book cover at least one aspect of how to successfully plug into the DNA of your organization.

Chapter 32

BE AN OBSERVER

Open your mind like a satellite to the stars and soak up the knowledge of the universe.

I was going through boxes of my stuff when I moved recently from Palo Alto to Los Angeles and I uncovered the above quote from a poem I wrote when I was a teenager. As I reread it, I thought of it as it applies to our work, and it really resonated with me. It speaks to this *Precision Prospect Development* process of getting plugged into the DNA of your environment, whether that be your department, your unit, your office, your organization, your technology, your school, your colleagues, or your industry. Take a step back from yourself and observe. Soak up your surroundings. Collect the data that surrounds you.

Quiet your mind. Empty your mind. Listen. Do this in a familiar environment. You will find that you will notice things that you've never noticed but have been in front of you for years. This is the best way to get to know what is really going on around you. ***If you don't know what is going on around you, how can you be sure that you are working on the right things? How can you know that your actionable intelligence is in fact actionable or intelligent?***

One of the goals of *Precision Prospect Development* is to get plugged into the DNA of your organization so that all activity can be in alignment with the movement of the organization while you simultaneously move the organization strategically forward with your *six elements*. The only way to do this is to have an intimate awareness of the makeup of each and every aspect of your organization.

The only way to achieve such awareness is to allow for a period of observation and data collection and to continue this process *ad infinitum*. Interact with all aspects of your office as an observer. Don't be afraid to put yourself out there. Schedule meetings with your stakeholders with the sole intent of learning as much as you can. Be like Johnny 5 from the movie, *Short Circuit* and gather, "Input! Input! Input!"

This is why it is so important to have a seat at the table. The more you know the better you can sharpen your tools and express your genius. You need to put yourself out there and gather data on all levels. The higher up you are able to go to gather data, the more you will understand what leadership wants and strategize on how to help influence the organization to exceed its goals.

Fill out your knowledge gaps. Ask about the goals of your constituents goals. Learn about the inner workings of their positions. Observation can be both passive and active. Pay extra special attention to the things that your constituents say. There are clues about how to best provide the most actionable intelligence floating all around you at the office, and sometimes the most valuable can come in casual conversation; you just have to know how to listen. You have to tune into the frequency of observation to hear. Allow your observations to guide you. Allow your observations to begin to fill up your data stores with the nuts and bolts necessary to build out your P*recision Prospect Development* program.

As you take that step back and observe, it is important that you remain open. Always challenge your assumptions. You don't know everything. You never know where that next great idea is going to come from. You never know when that next data element is going to come into your mind that solves a problem you've been thinking about for months; you never know where that next project is going to come from. Try to have an open mind to everything. Open up to all possibilities, to all viewpoints, to all potential solutions, to all potential projects. Be like a sponge and soak up the data around you. Truly plug in and remain open to the potential outputs/conclusions you come to through this process of observation. Try your best to remain detached from those conclusions so as not to sway your solutioning based on biases you may have.

If you don't touch your computer for a little while, what does it do? It goes into sleep mode and shuts off until you hit a button to turn it back on again. Don't go into sleep mode. Always be on. Always be open to any and every possibility. Don't be closed minded or closed off to other ways of doing things. Don't get trapped into the limited belief that there is only one way of doing things.

The more open you are, the more data you collect about your organization, and the better you will be able to deliver custom products and custom projects that will amaze your stakeholders and senior leadership. They will take notice that your work is plugged into the ethos. They will wonder how you are so spot-on with your projects. They will notice that you have impeccable timing. And then they will have to listen to you, they will have to come to you. They will become aware of your expertise and come to you more and more. Think a little bit about that.

An old saying my mom used to say when I was growing up was ***"you have two ears and one mouth for a reason. You should listen twice as much as you speak."*** Sometimes I will sit in a meeting and if I don't feel like I have something necessary to say, I won't say anything at all. I will sit and observe and write things in my notebook. I will soak up what is going on around me and file it away with the rest of my data, and what comes out as actionable I will take action on. I find that sometimes that it's more productive to be an observer in a meeting, than if I'm sitting there trying to have an ego battle with somebody or trying to show off how smart I am, and engaging in a jousting match of the minds, so to speak. Don't get sucked into that. Be an observer. Also, don't just wait for your turn to talk while others are speaking. When you are not speaking, listen and absorb what is being said.

Listening will not only get you far because of all of the data that it will allow you will collect and be able to incorporate into your department planning, and it will also increase your bonds with your stakeholders. Not very many people actually listen. We all want to be heard. To give someone that gift of being heard is a great thing. They will appreciate it. Their appreciation will help to forge your bond and increase your connection. With this increased connection, trust will grow stronger, and they will feel more and more comfortable opening up to you and telling you how they really feel.

As an observer, you need to get to this level of openness and transparency. The data that comes through this level of trusting connection will be most valuable in helping to set the course for action. You will learn more in depth what not to do, what they truly want, what bothers them and what they are thinking. Remember we are not in the service business, we are in the relationship, connection business. Get out of your office, and observe and connect.

Remember that since you are gathering data on a living, changing entity (your organization), don't forget that you must keep this process of observation ongoing indefinitely. As you embark on this journey of observation, make it a regular thing. Build in the practice of observation into your being, and it will become like second nature. As an active observer, you'll collect data no matter where you are or what you are doing and it will inform your decision making. It will keep you on track, and provide you with the raw materials necessary to stay in sync and deliver top notch actionable intelligence.

The below chart is a rough sketch of all of the different areas that you will want to gather as much data on as possible. The more data you gather on the below the better you will be able to align yourself with the DNA of your organization.

Organization	***Department***	***Employee***	***Donor***
Mission	Mission	Personality	Personas
Goal	Function	Function	Function
Make-up	Goals	Goals	Goals
Characteristics	Make-up	Characteristics	Characteristics
Culture	Characteristics	Culture	Pathways
Gift Opportunities	Culture	Business Processes	
Volunteers	Business Processes	Volunteers	
	Gift Opportunities		
	Volunteers		

Below is a copy of the full poem referenced in the beginning of this chapter that I wrote as a child:

From: Philosophy I.

When one has a closed mind, or a set of principles, which one believes in one's mind to be ultimately true, then one limits one's self to those principles. More importantly, one limits one's imagination to those principles, for when the process of imagining and thinking takes place, the thoughts and imaginings which go against one's set beliefs shall be thrown out more frequently at the subconscious level of the mind before they reach the conscious level. For when one believes in one's mind that one knows everything, or at least when one is under the assumption that the truths one holds at the moment are absolutely true and unshakeable, one places serious limitation upon the advancement of the soul. Through close-mindedness, one chokes one's imagination and other random thought processes. With restraints upon the imagination, new ideas and thoughts are not contemplated. Without the contemplation of new ideas and thoughts one remains idle upon the staircase of Truth. For a closed mind is like a prison to the soul.

Thus, one must open one's mind, and constantly examine one's principles and beliefs. For it is written, "The unexamined life is not worth living."

One must open one's mind so as not to block out the creative aspect of the mind, the imagination.

One must open up one's mind like a satellite to the stars, and soak up the knowledge of the universe.

Chapter 33

ANALYZE THE DATA

"Life can only be understood backwards; but it must be lived forwards."

Soren Kierkegaard

All of your observations should result in raw data that can be utilized to run a full analysis on your entire organization, including the functions of each department, the functions of each role, the inner workings of each individual, the mission of your organization, the various pathways of the donor experience, the culture of the office, the goals, the systems, the business processes, and more.[13] (See above chart for more.) The data you collect will make up the raw materials from which you can source your solutions. Make sure that you have gathered enough raw data through observation to run a proper analysis.

[13] See chart in Chapter 32 "Be an Observer"

Use multiple algorithms to run your analysis. This is vital because the results of your analysis are going to drive the activities of your department and your work. They will also drive your actions, your posture, and your behavior. You need to make sure that your analysis is spot-on so that you are always positioned for success.

As data people, we are natural at analysis. We are naturals at building systems based on data. We write algorithms to help us understand patterns in data. Lean on those skills and direct them at understanding the DNA of your organization as much as possible. Your analysis should result in a string of next-best actions that help to direct all activity of your department.[14] Your inner algorithms are at the core of your analysis, helping you case-by-case to always do the best thing that will produce the best outcome.

Your analysis should look for things like cause and effect. If I do x, y is the outcome. If I do z, b is the outcome. Observe through the actions and behaviors of others in your office. Look at the results of their actions. What did they do? What were the results of what they did? This is what you are analyzing. You are analyzing how the interplay of all *six elements* of all of the variables in the categories work together and interact with one another. Remember that the output of your analysis should be advice on what the *next best action* should be in any and every situation.

Remember that you are gathering data on a living, changing entity. Because of this, you must keep this process of observation and analysis ongoing indefinitely, for as long as you are at your organization. As new data comes through, funnel it through your analysis and allow your conclusions to change accordingly. Tweak your analysis algorithm so that it remains as up to date as possible and gives the most relevant options for action. Don't rest on your laurels. Don't stop scanning for changes.

---

[14] See Chapter 37 "Next Best Action"

Strategies and behaviors need to constantly evolve and change to ensure the greatest output. Just because something was of importance one day does not guarantee it will be of importance the next. Allow flexibility in your internal analytics, and change things up when your results are not what you thought they should be. Sometimes it's because you may have missed some important data elements to plug into your algorithm, and other times it is an adjustment that needs to be made in your algorithm.

We are already doing this at some level in order to survive as a living being. In order to do anything in your life you are running an analysis in the background that provides possible outputs. You choose an output and move forward. The trick is to make sure that you are efficiently operating with the appropriate algorithms, collecting enough data and evolving your algorithms over time so that you are in precision alignment with yourself and the outside world at all times.

The brain is a muscle and like any other muscle it grow stronger and sharper with use. The more you practice analyzing the observational dataset derived from six elements that surround you, the sharper your analysis algorithm will become. The more aware you are of the outcome of your choices, the more you will be able to tweak your analysis algorithm for more better and more precise results.

Input your observational data through multiple internal algorithms to spit out by ranking next best actions for every situation you are faced with.

Chapter 34

GET IN SYNC

Align yourself so closely with the DNA of your organization so that you can no longer tell where it begins and you end.

Once you have gathered enough data through observation and run it through your analysis algorithms, the next step is to get all of your activity in sync with the DNA of your organization. To get in alignment. Observation collects raw data; analysis develops solutions. Getting in sync ensures that the solutions are deployed with the proper adjustment to your *six elements* for maximum impact.

The process of getting into alignment is a lot like swimming or surfing in the ocean. You are probably aware that if you go out in the water and move against the tide or the flow of the waves, it can quickly zap your energy and you won't last long. If you fight against the current, you will be tossed back to shore, out of breath and out of energy. You really have to bend your will and align yourself with the movement of the ocean. You can't force the ocean to behave a certain way. You can't force it to get in alignment with you. Prior to getting into the water, you must first observe the movements of the ocean. You have to observe the waves, look for an undertow, get a sense of the mood of the ocean in that particular moment.

You then analyze your observations. The results of your analysis will inform you as to the best path to take to have the most enjoyable swimming experience or to catch the most waves. The next step is to jump in. Get in sync with the activity of the ocean. Instead of being thrown back to shore, out of breath, you'll be able to glide along with the current. You'll be able to harness the energy and power of the ocean to propel you forward and put you where you want to be. You'll use less energy and be able to swim longer.

The same goes for your activity with your organization. You can't force things to be a certain way; it will never work. If you try to exert your will too much, you'll get tossed back into your office. You have to get in precision alignment with all aspects of your organization in order to achieve success and maximize impact.

There is this element of taking your ego and your will out of the equation, or at least not allowing your will to dictate everything, especially in the face of an organization that is heading in a different direction. You must be willing to bend; flexibility is vital. If you can't bend, this process will break you. The key to proper alignment is striking the right balance between your energy and the energy of every element at your organization: mission, departments, leadership, technology and colleagues. This process is a give and take. This is why the iterative process is so important[15]. You are rarely ever going to get things right in your first try. You must be open to feedback from your colleagues and constituents at all times, and incorporate that data into your being and pivot as required for greater alignment and impact.

[15] See Chapter 54 "The Iterative Process"

As data folks, we are in a position of knowledge. Sometimes it can seem like our knowledge goes further than our constituents. Sometimes this can make us feel like we know best. Fight this urge. Rely heavily on the data you collected and analyzed about your organization, and make sure you are taking the *next best action* that will ensure successful outcomes.

Think about the hierarchy of your organization. Understand your hierarchy in your organization, and as you work with people, see where they stand in the hierarchy and make sure that you are not taxing them too much, or that you are sort of balancing where they are, and giving them the information based on their level. The information that you would give somebody at the top would look completely different than the information you give to somebody at the next rung, and the next rung, and the next rung. Understand the hierarchy and understand the types of information, and really customize everything so that you are giving custom information to everyone. You will have so much more influence and so much of a greater impact.

Aligning yourself will allow you to see what lies ahead. By seeing what is ahead, you can anticipate for future projects, and set the course for success. The more you are aligned the further you will be able to see. This foresight is vision. Having vision is worth its weight in gold. Your vantage point will be far greater than anyone else in your office causing you to have an edge. You can begin to exert your influence in a way that is seamless and in sync. If a big change is required, by being in sync, you are in the best position for you and your team to help steer the ship in a positive direction. Use your edge to benefit everyone in your office. Use this edge to help your organization raise more money, increase efficiencies, and optimize the donor experience. Do this and you will be indispensable for success. Use your vision to help ensure that your department and your organization are on the right course.

Chapter 35

IMPLEMENT WITH PRECISION

Human beings are the embodiment of precision.

You're an observer. You're an analyst, perfecting multiple internal algorithms simultaneously. You're in sync with the collective organization you are a part of. The next step is putting all of these together, keeping them operating at all times simultaneously, working in concert together to help you implement the *next best action* at all times in every way and in all things with precision. Welcome to the circus of life, you are on your way to becoming a master tight rope walker. A great master once said, "The world is a narrow bridge, the important thing is to not be afraid."[16]

[16] Nachman of Breslov

Every action has a reaction. What we do reverberates outward in ways we may never understand. Our actions should be under our control at all times. Keep your discipline and push your organization forward in a positive direction. Remember that; keep things positive at all times. Don't let distractions keep you away from landing your impact. Don't let others' negativity push you to express negativity back out into the world. Set your algorithm to discard distractions. Focus on the multitude of the *six elements* that surround you and use precision to move them in a way that will benefit everyone, not just yourself.

Make sure that you are running your possible actions through the filters of truth, compassion, positivity, and love. This will help to ensure that you're activity will not cause harm to others around you. If you exist on this level, your actions will reverberate in a positive direction, will build others up, and help others to achieve their greatness, as well.

Implementation is the tricky part but it will come with ease the more you observe, analyze and get in sync. ***After practice this entire system will become like second nature.*** It is already part of our natural makeup, and it is how you have survived long enough to be able to read these pages right now. Human beings are the embodiment of precision. Tap into your natural abilities and the natural energy of the physical world and move mountains, express your genius, actualize your potential. Doing so feels so good, and it is why we are here.

Chapter 36

THE IMPORTANCE OF INTUITION

Intuition

noun

> the ability to understand something immediately, without the need for conscious reasoning
>
> Google Dictionary

My understanding of intuition is that is does involve reasoning, but that that reasoning is happening on a layer within our minds that we are not consciously aware of. As you begin to embody this system of alignment and get in the flow with your collective organization, you will operate at times on a level that might be labeled intuition. As you put everything together and implement with precision, you might not always understand why certain *next best action*s are being recommended, or why certain beliefs or positions begin to take hold. This is ok. Don't be afraid of empowering yourself with this extra ability of being able to intuitively make decisions that are in alignment with the collective organization.

Intuition is an algorithm just like any other, only that it operates more like an unsupervised model more than a supervised model. It is harder to unpack the reasoning as the rationale is usually beyond what our minds are capable of understanding.

When you operate in this precision method, your intuition will be more rooted in reality and will be more accurate. You will be strengthening this muscle, along with the muscle of observation and analysis. You will constantly be in a state of becoming an even better employee and colleague. Your ability to observe will increase in power and so will your ability to properly analyze. You're internal algorithms will become more accurate and precise. Your ability to implement will grow sharper, as well. Keep in mind that this is not perfect, and that perfection is not the goal.

Once you have been practicing this for a while, don't be afraid to include intuition into your repertoire. It is a natural outcome of this process anyway. Even if you try to ignore it, you won't be able to. You may get red flags when dealing with folks in the back of your mind saying don't trust this person. When this is the case, tread more cautiously when around that person. It may show up in many forms, from protecting you and your team and the collective organization, to showing up to help you choose the right project. Either way, it will be a helpful guide; when precision tunes into reality, it is a powerful tool for creativity and actualizing amazing things into existence.

Intuition can help you to actualize something that you may not have been able to actualize with your rational mind. It is important to have this integrated into your system. Some of the most brilliant things you will do will be born from your intuition. ***All of the data that you are collecting and the skills that you are sharpening will help your intuition to be more reliable.***

Chapter 37

NEXT BEST ACTION

The path to achieving your goals is lined by a string of next best actions.

The *next best action* is the most-strategic action that can be taken in any given moment that will get you closest to achieving your goal and/or have the best outcome. For our purposes, we can group the term into two buckets.

1. The *next best action* that will help you and your team to achieve impact at your organization. We can think of these as internal *next best action*s.
2. The *next best action* that can be taken by your constituents to enhance the donor experience, result in more gifts, and help to fulfill the mission of your organization. We can think of these as external *next best action*s.

Next Best Action vs. Actionable Intelligence

*Next best action*s are different from actionable intelligence. Not every *next best action* will contain actionable intelligence. *Next best action*s direct activity from a micro to a macro level. Actionable intelligence is one of our products. We are service providers. One of our main services is providing intel that is actionable. Actionable intelligence refers to that part of your work that prompts action by your constituents.

Internal Next Best Actions

The results of your internal algorithms processing all of the data you collect as an observer will result in a string of next best actions. You will always have to choose which path to take. There will be very few (if any) times where you are faced with only one internal *next best action.* Everything we do is the result of choosing an internal *next best action.* Many of these decisions are on autopilot and are not consciously made. In the office setting, our work-related actions determine our future path.

Due to the chaotic nature of existence, we must remain vigilant and make sure that at work we are always doing our best to put our best foot forward and make the *next best action* that is going to serve the collective. Not everyone operates this way, though, and most direct their activity to benefit themselves. This is a shame, and I do not want anyone to use this system for ego or personal glory. ***This system is only meant for those who care about others, care about the collective organisms that they are a part of, and seek to do what is right for the collective organization.*** Due to the way that our organizations are set up, sometimes self-preserving behavior takes hold out of fear. Try not to let fear turn you into a selfish monster. Don't accept people at face value; often it is those who pretend to be service oriented who are the least interested in service of others. Be careful where you hang your hat. Don't be afraid to take yourself out of a bad situation.

As you walk through your day at work, you will be constantly be faced with decisions to make. Those decisions will be made by picking a *next best action* from a list of internal recommendations. The data you gather as an observer informs your internal algorithms. Those algorithms spit out possible *next best action*s in order of highest likelihood for success. The data that is gathered from being plugged in will help you to make these decisions and choose the right one in every situation.

External Next best actions

One of our outputs is *actionable intelligence.* This is intelligence that prompts action by our constituents, and helps to inform our constituents to take the *next best action* with their prospects to unlock gifts. Let's say you are a fundraiser and you have a prospect that you are attempting to meet with. In this instance, your goal is to get a meeting. Your external *next best action* at any given moment will be whatever is going to help you to get closer to the meeting.

Our work should be around building a platform to operate in a way to constantly direct the development officers to their *next best action*s. The ultimate in actionable intelligence is that which gives birth to the right *next best action* at the right time. Ultimately, we want to have our platform give recommendations on the *next best action* for all prospects in our database to increase revenue, enhance the donor experience, and fulfill your organization's mission.

One of my weaknesses is that I tend to go quiet when I do not have enough data collected about the *six elements* around me at any given moment. If I don't have enough data to know what my *next best action* is, I don't get a recommendation at all, and I am silent. This doesn't always work out well for me and sometimes puts me in a bad place, because I need to wait until I get the answer or have a *next best action* to complete. This is a flaw of this system; it is usually only apparent though when in a newer surrounding that does not feel safe. My internal algorithm says errors in action could result in bad consequences, so silence is preferred to taking a wrong action based on sparse data. This is also why safety and trust are so vital. The more safe an environment more readily employees will express their genius without fear or inhibition.

Chapter 38

THE ELEMENT OF INWARDNESS

"The aim of art is to represent, not the outward appearance of things, but their inward significance."

Aristotle

Self-reflection is absolutely vital for the survival of any living human being. As you practice the process of observation, analyzing, getting in sync, and implementing with precision for success, your skills in each area will grow exponentially. You'll become an acute observer with vision and start noticing things you never noticed before; your analysis and internal algorithms will be so sharp and precise that you'll be making decisions with more precision; folks in your office may start to wonder if you have some sort of sixth sense.

You must not only look out to your organization, but must also practice your observational skills on yourself. Take this same process as outlined above and focus it internally on yourself to better yourself. Apply this same process to yourself aimed at helping you on your road to becoming. You must turn your observations inward, and apply the same principles to your own collective. You must consciously plug into your own DNA in order to ensure the best outcome in all situations for everyone. As you point your observation skills inward, you must also point your analytical skills inward. You must analyze yourself, not only as the role you play in the collective of your organization, but how you are as a being.

This internalizing of things and pointing inward will allow you to burn off inefficiencies and bad habits that are not serving you or your organization. This self-reflective work must happen at the same time that you are working to get in alignment with your collective organization; the self-reflective work should focus on getting you in alignment with yourself and the truth. Look at yourself through the lenses of truth, compassion, positivity and love, and set your algorithms to ensure that you operate in a way that leaves all beings that you encounter better off after an encounter with you rather than worse. Look within, and ensure that you are not aligning with bad behaviors, like hurting people or stealing the work and creativity of others.

As you push to help your collective organization grow, make sure you are also growing in the process and evolving alongside it. The more you are evolved internally, the easier it will be to ensure a positive outcome when faced with difficult work situations.

In the words of Abraham Joshua Heschel, "**The meaning of life is to build life as if it were a work of art.** You're not a machine. When you're young start working on this great work of art called your own existence... Remember the importance of self-discipline… Study the great sources of wisdom... Remember that life is a celebration… what's really important is life as celebration."

Chapter 39

THE IMPORTANCE OF CHANGE

"How can I be sure, in a world that's constantly changing? How can I be sure?.... I really, really, really want to know!"

Young Rascals,
How Can I Be Sure

Our existence is such that we are constantly being born again at every moment. Change is the essence of life. Who we are now is not who we will be tomorrow. As the existentialists say, we are constantly in a state of becoming. At all times we are in flux, changing, malleable, unfolding, and growing. The changing nature of life provides us with all of the opportunities we need to build great things and succeed in our jobs. Change provides the pathways and space for our greatest potentials to become actualized. Change is why we must always be alert and remain aware. Change is why we must continuously, without pause, and simultaneously be an observer and analyst to inform our synchronization and implementation strategies.

There is an ancient story about one of the Buddhas that may help shed some light on this. One day, as the Buddha sat in front of his disciples, instead of giving a talk, as was his usual routine, all he did was hold up a flower. Instantly one of his disciples attained enlightenment. I've always been amazed by this story and been in awe at the power of that moment. While I have yet to achieve enlightenment by looking at a flower, my takeaway from this story is that if you remain open to change, in the flash of an instant, even when you least expect it, you can change so much, your entire worldview can shift so dramatically, to the point that you are unrecognizable from one instant to the next, while remaining the same person.

This is what's so great about the changing nature of existence, that's what's so cool about being infinite in the finite. We are alive because of change, we are able to move, to think, to speak, to eat, laugh, cry, and love all because of change. ***Change is something to be grateful for, not to fear. Embrace it.***

Don't pay attention to those who try to look down on you or make you feel inferior or inauthentic because you change your opinion or strategy or beliefs. They have a negative word that they use in political culture to try and discredit someone whose opinions have evolved. They call it the 'flip flop,' and try to denounce anyone who changes. Think about this for a minute. Is it really bad to change your opinion? If you are the same person you were last month, then you're not learning enough; you're not challenging yourself, you're not growing. ***Without change, you stagnate like a pool of still water.*** When you are stagnate, you are in danger of becoming overridden by toxic bacteria. You don't want stagnation. Instead, you want to live a life of movement like a river, ever-changing as you flow, leaving sediment behind as you hit against the rocks, becoming more and more distilled and pure so that someone can drink from the fountain of your essence and become refreshed rather than poisoned.

Given the fact that change is the essence of life, you would think that we would be used to change by now, and adept at adopting and adapting to our ever-changing environment. We should be able to eat change for breakfast. On a base level, we are really good at adjusting to change. It is built into our system for survival. But this is not always the case in the workplace. This office environment is still a new thing for us, and we have not yet evolved enough to incorporate this into our seamless change category. Of all of the places where change can occur, there is nothing more frightening or that can cause as much anxiety as change in the workplace. But this is also the place that requires the most change for success.

We have already established that our organizations are living collective entities. As living entities, our organizations will constantly change. Our organizations are constantly in a state of becoming, thus the importance of aligning yourself with the DNA of your organization so that the changes come seamlessly for you.

Harness the power of change to actualize as much of your potential as possible. When one of your previous projects becomes obsolete, don't see it as a failure; use it as an opportunity to fill the gap with something even better, even more impactful. Don't get stuck on the fact that it is no longer being adopted or having the ROI that it once had. See this as a blessing and opportunity for something even better because that is exactly what it is. It is not a failure of your work, it is the natural outcome of our work. The more you cling to, and/or get hung up on the difference between today and tomorrow and allow that to blind you from the opportunities that are presented in the present, the less successful you will be.

We all have things that we want to do and projects that we want to work on, but sometimes the timing isn't right. It might be that a change in organizational strategy or focus is necessary to open up the opportunity for that project to take place. It might require a change in you and your strategy. There is a common saying that success happens when opportunity meets preparedness. Make sure that you are prepared with a strategy to implement when change opens up a window of opportunity to move forward. Remain patient until change creates opportunity for the actualization of project potential. Do your part to usher in that change as much as you can while remaining positive. Stay in tune with your organization's DNA, and implement according to the changing tides.

There are two things about change that are important to keep in perspective and can help to create a more accepting relationship between yourself and change:

1. When something you enjoy, like, or perceive as pleasant changes, make sure that you don't become too attached or cling on to the things that you like or perceive as pleasant. This will only set you up for disappointment, as there will likely come a time when these things go away. It is important for this reason to keep a healthy level of detachment from the things you enjoy. The majority of the work that we do has a shelf life. The shelf-life can be rather short. We have to remain clear and not allow for our attachment to our projects prevent us from moving on or iterating when the time for change is upon us.

2. When something you don't enjoy, don't like or perceive or as painful changes, make sure that you don't become too stressed out or bothered. What you don't like or what is perceived as painful also has a shelf life, and will eventually cease to exist. Keep this in mind when something or someone is rattling you at work. Don't get sucked into that world. Remind yourself that this too shall pass and move on.

In part, we fear change because change reminds us of our own impermanence. Every time something changes, our subconscious is like, "Omg, just like this thing no longer exists, so too at some point we will no longer exist. Yikes. This is scary." This brings on a fear response and causes us to cling to things that we should instead be letting go of.

If we remain in a static environment with minimal change, we can gain a stronger sense of security at the subconscious level about our own existence. A feeling of safety and security overcomes us. The irony is that we don't notice that we are actually stagnating and dying instead of actually living.

Change is life. Stagnation is death. An improper relationship with self and change will cause this fear response to limit your growth and put you in a state of hibernation until the day comes when you actually do pass on. Stagnation is not safety. Getting too comfortable in an unchanging state will cause you to prematurely enter the state that you fear most which is the state where you can no longer change. This is kind of a paradox. This is why practicing the art of detachment is so important. Never fear change, embrace it. It is a reminder that you are alive. It is a reminder that you can change the things around you, that you can change yourself, your situation, your beliefs, your job, your focus. Trust in yourself and the universe that you will be ok no matter what change befalls you. Everything will be ok.

A changing work environment is healthy. It is unavoidable. Embrace this. If the right changes are being made at the right time, it will increase success and allow your organization to grow and further fulfill its mission and create the ultimate experience for your donors. As your organization changes, change with it. Align yourself with the flow and position yourself as an influencer so that you can have an impact on where, when and how your organization changes. Seize every opportunity that change opens up for you. Be vigilant about this. ***Be on the lookout always for opportunities that change presents to you.*** Every day is so different from the next, you can sometimes make what was impossible one day, an actuality the next. Don't ever close off to possibility and change.

Chapter 40

CONSTANTLY REFRESH YOUR DATA

"Thoroughly unprepared, we take the step into the afternoon of life. Worse still, we take this step with the false presupposition that our truths and our ideals will serve us as hitherto. But we cannot live the afternoon of life according to the program of life's morning, for what was great in the morning will be little at evening and what in the morning was true, at evening will have become a lie."

Carl Jung

The above quote by Carl Jung is quite remarkable and imparts such a fundamental truth. The essence of life is change. Given that the essence of life is change, what might be true in the morning might not be true in the evening. What was untrue in the morning might have become truth by evening. We must live in the moment. Our activity must be dictated by the data of the moment, the present conditions as informed by the past, and looking out to the future. Just because something was of great importance and focus at one moment, doesn't mean it will hold the same weight in the next. You must pay attention to what the data is telling you so that you can operate in alignment with what each moment calls for. If you can master this concept, your success rate will skyrocket.

When applied as a business principle this means that you must constantly refresh your data to ensure that you are not operating on conclusions derived from false, out of date, data. You must always be ready to change things up, pivot on a dime. ***Plug into the DNA of your organization so that when the strategic direction shifts, your department's focus shifts with it.*** Keep your mind open and observations running constantly. ***Set up your internal algorithms to alert you when the conditions have changed in favor of your work.***

We often approach our business processes as if they will always work. Many folks get caught in the mindset that the way things have always been done in the past will always be superior to any new method because the historical way of doing things has proven to work thus far. This is a false presupposition. This is a misunderstanding of the phrase "If it isn't broke, don't fix it." The process might still work, but that doesn't mean that it is still the best process to continue to implement.

As data folks, we should be acutely aware of this principle. We refresh data on a daily basis as a routine task of our jobs. If we don't run a refresh, we will provide inaccurate information in our spreadsheets and reports. This is unacceptable and we would never knowingly deliver a report with out of date data. We would never skip the step of refreshing the date before delivering the report. We should also apply this principle to all of our activities.

We know that we rarely, if ever, have the complete picture on anything that we analyze or work on. There is always some data missing, and the variables are constantly moving. Sometimes you know what data is missing, but most of the time you don't even know what additional data exists that you're not capturing. We do the best analyses we can based on the available data we have at the time. When we discover new data, or that data has changed, we incorporate it into our analysis. When we receive this new data, our conclusions can change. We have to be ready to pivot and change as the data suggests, and not cling to previously held beliefs or decisions; otherwise we will make the wrong choices, constrained by our inability to embrace change. We have to throw out our static models and adopt machine learning so that our analytics stay current with the changes in the data of our prospects.

When you approach your job this way--your life this way--you will find that you have a lot less static, it will be a lot smoother sailing, and your success rate will greatly increase. Again, this is another just really important lesson as you move along your path and in your career. Be aware and be sensitive to the changing nature of life; be as plugged in as possible to your culture, your DNA, and the changing priorities of leaderships. This takes time, discipline and energy. It requires an extra exertion of energy to remain on the alert for changing conditions.

One day leadership may say this is the goal and the next day they may say, wait, no, *this* is the goal. They might not make it so obvious by saying it directly but if you are plugged into the DNA of your office, you should be able to notice when shifts like this occur. Make sure you are on that journey with them, that you are out there, and you have your ears out there; that you open up your mind like a satellite to the stars and soak up the knowledge of the universe.

If you direct this principle at our prospecting and fundraising efforts, it reveals a fundamental truth: Just because someone is a prospect today doesn't mean that they will be a prospect tomorrow. Just because someone wasn't a prospect yesterday doesn't mean they are not a prospect today. Make sure that you are setting up your prospecting systems to account for this.

Don't allow the limited experience of one fundraiser's interactions with a prospect dictate all future interactions, or lack thereof. Maintain the ability to track a prospect's engagement with your organization beyond fundraiser activity. If they continue to show signs of interest, put them back into the pool and match them with another fundraiser to see if they are able to successfully engage the prospect in a manner that the prospect will respond positively to.

I remember very vividly when I built a portfolio for a new major gift fundraiser. I was excited by all of the great prospects I was able to find and assemble into this portfolio. We were actually able to hire this fundraiser because I had built out this portfolio and I recommended to my boss, the Chief Philanthropy Officer, that we needed to hire someone to cover it. I couldn't wait for this new fundraiser to start, to begin engaging with these prospects, and bring in gifts. I also couldn't wait for them to see how great their portfolio was and to receive the positive feedback.

I walked confidently into our first 1:1, only to be met with disappointment and fear. The fundraiser started talking discouragingly immediately, holding a printout of his entire portfolio. He asked me flat out, "What are you giving me here? Is this really my portfolio?" He wasn't happy. Confused and with my mind racing, I replied back, "Yeah it is. There are so many great prospects in there, I can't wait to see what you are able to do with them."

This didn't seem to help the situation. He said, "I've met with all of the other fundraisers, and we went through my portfolio together, and they all basically unanimously agreed that I have the worst portfolio. Ever." He said that each person pretty much pointed out a ton of names of prospects that were never going to give for this or that reason. He started to get visibly nervous and asked me "What should I do here? You're telling me this is good, and they are telling me that this is bad. I'm kind of scared here and not feeling very confident about my success."

He was in a new job and was a go getter. I could tell he was a performer. I had to think of something quick to alleviate his fears and get him back into a place of positivity, or else I knew he would never be able to fundraise to his highest potential. I thought, *potential*, yes, that's it. I replied, "You know, ***a fundraiser's portfolio exists at all times as pure potential. It is only as good as the fundraiser who staffs it.*** I don't know exactly what they told you about the names on this list, but what I do know is that the data is telling me that this is an amazing list of prospects, and that there are a ton of gifts in here waiting for you to get them. I wouldn't have put bad names in here. Don't listen to them. Keep your beginner's mind as long as you can. Don't allow their experiences or beliefs to impact yours in a negative way. You got this. They are wrong. Trust me. This is a great portfolio."

Three months later, he received a seven figure gift from one of those prospects that the others said would never give. A few months after that, he received another seven figure gift, then a five, then a seven. He was the most successful fundraiser from a revenue standpoint that year. If he had trusted in the old, obsolete data of his peers, he never would have raised a single dime that year, as all of his gifts were from names they had deemed not viable prospects. It was ironic because later, the other fundraisers came to me and asked me to give them a portfolio like this new fundraiser's because 'he has all the good prospects.' To which I would smile and say "Sure thing. How many do you need?"

Change opens the doors to new possibilities. Don't be discouraged by a no or by a situation that does not go in your favor. One of the best ways to harness this is to constantly refresh your data and adjust according. Stay nimble and flexible so that change does not break you. Learn from the lessons that previous data refreshes teach you about the art of aligning with your organization's DNA. Be prepared to implement a given project or strategy as soon as changing variables open up the window of opportunity. Most importantly, enjoy the ride. This process is actually a lot of fun and rewarding.

Chapter 41

SPEAK THE LANGUAGE OF YOUR CONSTITUENTS AND PLAY TO THEM

"I guess you guys are not ready for that yet…
but your kids are gonna love it."

Marty McFly,
Back to the Future

The above quote is taken from that scene in *Back to the Future* when Marty picks up the guitar and joins the band on stage at his parents' high school dance back in 1955. Rock n roll was in its early stages at the time. He plays the 1958 Chuck Berry song *Johnny B. Goode*, which doesn't exist yet. This is a new sound to the crowd; they are a little curious at first, but they all like it and jump right in, and everyone is having a great time. The band is really jamming, and the students are dancing. As Marty gets into the song more and more, he starts jumping around the stage and taking the rock part further and further, and starts doing more and more of an 80s rock/metal version of the song, crawling around the stage with 80s moves. As he goes further and further off track and into the future of music, one by one, he loses each member of the band.

They basically stop playing their instruments and just stare, dumbfounded. This goes on until Marty is the only one playing on stage. He is so into it, by this point his eyes are closed (he is completely closed off to his audience and his bandmates) that he is totally unaware that he lost them. When he finally finishes, he opens his eyes and the entire crowd is standing still, staring at him. This is a great analogy that illustrates a lot of the concepts in this book.

I am sure many of you have felt like Marty McFly in that scene at certain points in your career. I know I have. You are jamming out some complicated reports with complicated logic, and you're presenting them to fundraisers. You think you are on a roll. You may or may not have them in the beginning. You know what you are doing is highly advanced data work and you're excited to share it. You're throwing out all of these advanced, technical terms and it feels good.

Yet instead of being greeted by smiling faces and applause, you're greeted with blank stares. Instead of the reports having a positive impact, they have little to no impact at all. Instead of the fundraisers wanting to learn more and wanting more of your time, they want less, and are looking at the clock so that they can make their escape. When this happens to me it is an especially tough pill to swallow because it is usually when I am engaging in something that I am passionate about.

I've heard countless of times from data folks, "Oh, they are just not ready; they just don't understand." But is that what the problem really is here? This reaction may help us to take away the sting of rejection, but you don't want to put the sole blame on your audience. Yes there may be sometimes when your audience is unfair but that is not always the case.

When you deliver a project or some actionable intelligence, you want your constituents to be like "Woo-Hoo!" You want to knock it out of the park. You want your constituents to be in sync with you at all times, and you want to be in sync with them. You want to speak their language at all times, peppering in some of yours so as to expand their vocabulary.

In order to truly maser Precision Prospect Development, you must be a master linguist. At a minimum, you must be able to speak the language of data, and you must also be able to speak the language of fundraising. Ideally, you must be able to speak the individual language of each and every single one of your constituents. You must be able to go back and forth from one language to another at the drop of a hat; you must be able to communicate clearly and effectively with all constituents in their language of choice. ***You must be able to transition from data to philanthropy; you must be able to convey your work in simple terms, in the language of your audience.***

If you are in front of senior leadership giving a presentation, you must speak leadership speak. If you are in a major gifts strategy meeting, you must speak major gifts strategy speak. There is different vocabulary for these situations. It even goes beyond the spoken word to include body language, demeanor, dress, and tone. If you try to force your language on them, it will backfire. They won't understand. The goal is to deliver actionable intelligence in a language they understand so that they can take action. If someone speaks French, you wouldn't give them a book written in English, and expect them to be able to have a conversation about plot and character based on the book.

In speaking the language of your constituents and playing projects to them, at their level, you're actually helping to increase their data vocabulary. This might seem counter-intuitive, but it's true. It works. I think what holds some of us back from taking the time to go out of our way to learn their language and to make sure to meet them on their level is that we think this will go on forever and be a big inconvenience, but this is not the case.

The more you invest in speaking their language, the more they will learn yours. They will actually pick up more and more of your language and begin to have those ah – ha moments. They will begin to understand more and more data concepts, follow what is going on, and understand how it can be helpful for them. ***As their vocabulary expands, the gap between your language and theirs will shrink***; as the gap shrinks, you will get more and more in sync; as you get more in sync, you will produce better work. With better work, comes better results.

Remember the goal is to make sure that your actionable intelligence is acted upon. If this means you have to exert extra effort to ensure this happens, then this will always be time well spent. This time ensuring that action takes place is more valuable than working on another project. If you don't go that extra step, to ensure buy-in and action, it will negate all of the work that you did to begin with.

In order to speak multiple languages, you must be able to master the art of distilling the complex into its simple parts. ***You must be able to take complicated technical concepts, simplify them, and put them into general terms.*** This is a skill in and of itself. Anyone can do it; it just requires effort. But if you master this, you are on your way to being able to speak the language of anyone you encounter in life, because ***the language of simplicity is the universal language.*** If you are unsure of the precise language of your audience or constituents, you should always defer to the language of the simple.

The mind is a wonderfully complicated instrument with all kinds of wiring that we haven't even begun to understand. One thing that we do know, is that the mind is made up of neural pathways. Neural pathways are developed as you learn and grow. As you learn new skills, new neural pathways and connections are made. Remember, the brain is a muscle and it grows stronger with use. ***Help your constituents exercise the linguistic and comprehension muscles in their brain and they will become weight bearing in areas where they were previously weak.*** This can be slow-moving process. It can take some time for these to develop, and it will require a certain amount of repetition. It also requires exposure at a digestible level.

By speaking the language of your constituents and translating

your data talk into their language, you are creating the perfect environment to nurture and grow new neural pathways for both yourself and your constituents. As these neural pathways take root and are strengthened, the language barrier is lessened; the knowledge gap is shortened. By approaching it this way, it ensures that these new neural pathways can be cultivated and nurtured and remain intact week after week.

If you've lived in a city your entire life, you likely won't need a map to get to the local store. You probably did the first few times, but after practice and repetition you no longer need the map. The database is a lot like a city, and the fields of a database are a lot like landmarks of a city.

It will take time for someone new to get acquainted with the streets and structure of your database. It will require patience and repetition. A lot of the work that we do for our constituents will seem foreign to them at first. It is our responsibility to make sure that we properly translate and deliver work to them so that they can understand and take action. If you are not doing this now, then you need to start ASAP.

Always remember, the language of simplicity is the universal language.

Chapter 42

ATTITUDE VS APTITUDE

Attitude is one of the filters through which our unbounded pure potential flows on its way to becoming activated in the present moment.

Do you enjoy working with a difficult coworker? When you see someone walking in your direction with a disagreeable temperament, do you walk in the other direction? If you have a question and need some help, but the person who has the solution is condescending and rude, do you sometimes just move on without attempting to get an answer to avoid having to deal with negativity, or go to someone else? Have you ever been in a meeting where one negative attitude can derail the entire creative process and prevent your team from flying?

There is nothing more disruptive than a colleague with a bad attitude. The impact of negativity can be exponential and derail, not only an entire team, but an entire organization. In short, it is bad for business. Have no tolerance for this on your team, and, more importantly, have no tolerance of this from yourself. Negativity is the biggest waste of time, and can create an exponential loss in productivity. Cultures based on negativity are destructive forces and should be avoided at all costs. Managers who operate on fear should be avoided.

If I had to choose between attitude and aptitude, I would choose attitude every time. Having the right attitude can advance a team more than someone with high aptitude and a bad attitude. There was a recent study that surveyed over 500 business leaders around the globe that asked a similar question; a resounding 78% chose personality as the key driver for a successful employee over anything else.

As mentioned in the intro, Google did a study in 2013 on some of its employee data called Project Oxygen. They analyzed all of their hiring and performance data, looking to hone in on the characteristics that made for the best employees. To the surprise of Google, technical skills, or STEM skills, were the least-important indicators of success, whereas all of the top characteristics for success were soft skills, like being a good listener, having compassion and empathy.

An exceptional attitude is something that senior leadership really wants to see, and will really reward you for. They will reward you for the right attitude and doing good work, more than rewarding you for being a total jerk and doing an amazing job.

As service providers, we want folks to want to work with us. The more that they want to come to us and can ask us for our opinion, the more we get to show off how super smart we are and how much value we bring to the table. The more projects we get to work on, the greater impact we can have.

Attitude is one of the filters through which our unbounded pure potential flows on its way to becoming activated in the present moment. It is one of the filters that dictate *how* we present ourselves in any given moment. Attitude is a large force in dictating our *how factor.*[17]

---

[17] See chapter on How vs What

As data folks, we are constantly called upon to find solutions to the problems of our stakeholders. We need to remain as free and open as possible to all solutions. The more we are open and clear in our solutioning, the better our solutions will be. Given this fact, it is even more vital to approach our work with a positive attitude. Not only do we rely on strong relationships for success, we rely on our ability to remain focused and positive when faced with difficult challenges, and must harness that positivity to find solutions where others have failed.

The right attitude can be the difference between finding the right solution for a problem versus not. I have seen that when my employees approach their work with a bad attitude, it blinds them from the solution. It prevents them from doing their best and from delivering solutions, and instead they deliver disappointment. Continual delivery of disappointment sets off a vicious cycle, and the next thing you know, you're trapped on a hamster wheel of failure. The more you fail, the more your bad attitude is fed; the more it is fed, the stronger it becomes; the stronger it becomes, the more it breeds failure.

If you're having a bad day or are in a bad mood, try to keep your attitude in check until it clears. Try not to let it affect those around you in a negative way. Maybe just step out of the office for a little bit, or take a mental health day; get it out of your system, and then come back in with a smile.

If you find yourself in a job or a role that is causing you to consistently have a bad attitude, perhaps it is time to move on. Don't do it to yourself and don't do it to those around you. Life is too short. We spend too much time at work to spend it with people with bad attitudes. If you don't respect your constituents and can't come to a space mentally where you can respect them, then you either need to request new constituents to support, or move on to another organization.

Every time I've witnessed a person with a bad attitude move on for another opportunity, there is always this sigh of relief that takes place around the office; there is a collective, "Whew! Oh my gosh, that person was tough to be around." The atmosphere becomes lighter, more work gets done, more people are smiling, and creativity flows freely. It doesn't mean that they are bad people per se, but just that their behavior is highly disruptive to the functioning of a team. This behavior is also not healthy. It can create an environment of fear. No one wants to be around a downer who gives off the impression that they could lose their cool at any moment. And interacting with folks like this can take a toll. I have worked with people like this and have had employees like this on my team and the experience of working alongside them is anything but professional.

Work on your attitude. Use your highly refined algorithms to work together simultaneously to reflect on your attitude and make sure that you are not the bad apple that is spoiling the bunch. Approach your work with a healthy positive attitude that anything can be accomplished. Think big. Attitude is so closely tied to belief that this is one of your last filters through which the creative process flows through on its way to actualization. This means that the world that you create for yourself will hinge on your attitude. If you're not happy with your situation sometimes a shift in attitude is all it takes to achieve more palatable results.

Chapter 43

EMOTIONAL INTELLIGENCE

emotional intelligence

noun

> the capacity to be aware of, control, and express one's emotions, and to handle interpersonal relationships judiciously and empathetically

Google Dictionary

Emotional Intelligence is important for successful navigation of the work world. Your EQ score is like your IQ score, except it measures your capacity to control and express your emotions rather than your capacity for knowledge. Pay attention to your EQ. Invest in your emotional strength and well-being. Your EQ is just as important as your IQ. If you have a high EQ and you can control your emotions, you will have a much easier time navigating all of the potential pitfalls in your office. You will be able to deal with a difficult constituent or colleague with compassion and empathy. You will not allow difficult situations to rattle you.

If you are able to remain calm through storms, don't overreact, don't get involved in petty squabbles, and maintain positivity, you will be a highly-valued employee. High EQ is one of the top qualities that managers equate with success. If you are a high-performing employee with a high EQ, you are a dream employee for senior leadership. You will be rewarded for this in ways you could never have imagined.

This chapter is only meant to put this concept on your radar as an important aspect for success. For a deeper dive on this subject, check out some of the work of Dr. Travis Bradberry, one of the world's leading experts on Emotional Intelligence.

Chapter 44

TRUST & SAFETY

"The world is a narrow bridge, the essential thing is to not be afraid."

Rebbe Nachman of Breslov

Throughout all of this work, it is important that you also cultivate an atmosphere of safety and trust for you, your team, and the employees at your organization. Many problems, inefficiencies, and distractions are rooted in fear. Fear tends to be a combination of memories of bad experiences, plus thoughts of unknown future experiences that await us.

There are many fears that can plague one in an office setting. We can fear the loss of a job, stepping on someone's toes, rocking the boat, making an error, hurting someone's feelings, having our feelings hurt, embarrassment, a difficult colleague, being thrown under the bus, the spotlight, being alone. There are many things that can cause fear in someone. The more we can dispel fear from ourselves and operate from a place of acceptance and confidence, the more we will be able to express ourselves and operate at our highest potential.

Allow room for your employees and colleagues to make mistakes and try new things without fear of reprisal. Reward risk taking. We spend too much of our time in the office and with our colleagues for fear and distrust to dominate the environment. It can wear us down, decrease our productivity, and cause health problems. As you interact with those on your team and around your office, make sure that your interactions cultivate a cordial, collaborative office environment. Dispel fear when you encounter it, and support those around you so that their confidence levels increase.

Try your best to cultivate trust in the universe and trust in yourself that, even if something seemingly negative were to befall you, it will not break you, but will instead make room for something better to happen in your life. Sometimes it is hard to maintain this belief because as we look outside of ourselves and onto the world around us; there are so many instances where it appears that the universe is not taking care of other living beings.

Try not to allow these observations to eat away at your own belief that the universe will take care of you. ***Trust that no matter what obstacle you face, you will be able to overcome it.*** Trust that no matter what happens in your life, it all will have happened to push you forward, and end up working out in a positive way. Sometimes it may takes longer for the positive outcome to reveal itself, but given due time, it will.

There is something freeing in knowing that you are safe. Even if your manager or office does not cultivate an atmosphere of trust and safety, you can trust in yourself and the universe and know that you are safe. No one has any power over you or your life. The belief that they do is what causes the illusion that they do. Do not allow this belief to enter your mind. Move forward with the belief that you are safe no matter what.

As service providers, we want our constituents to feel safe when they work with us. Through fostering a safe, positive, work environment for our constituents, our relationships will become stronger. The stronger our relationships, the more they will share with us; the more they share with us about what they are working on, what their goals are, what they need form us, the more we can deliver precisely what they need to be successful; the more we deliver success, the more they will want to partner with us, and the more we can deliver success. As this process continues, solid bonds of trust, safety, and comradery continue to strengthen.

The atmosphere of our office is of primary importance for producing positive outcomes. Having a safe office culture where trust abounds is good for the bottom line. It is good for everyone all around. Managers who sow discord believing that that keeps people on their toes and produces better results have it all wrong. Do your part in creating a safe space so that everyone enjoys the freedom of expression and creativity in as unbounded way as possible. Such expressions are the ultimate forms of beauty.

Chapter 45

IMPERMANENCE AND HEALTHY DETACHMENT

"It is not impermanence that makes us suffer. What makes us suffer is wanting things to be permanent when they are not."

Nhat Hanh

In Buddhist tradition, the concept of impermanence permeates everything. There are many rituals and teachings dedicated to demonstrating impermanence. One in particular deals with the creation and destruction of a sand mandala. Mandala is a Sanskrit word that literally means "circle" and represents the universe. The sand mandala ritual takes place when Buddhist practitioners create intricate representations of the universe out of colorful sand.

They can spend months, sometimes years, building these super intricate designs out of sand. They are beautiful, intricate, masterful works of art that could go on display in any museum anywhere around the world.

But instead of sealing them off and keeping them for display, they ritualistically brush them away. They get a broom out and sweep it away. Even though they spend months or years building these amazing, intricate works of art filled with symbolism and meaning, they remain detached.

Historically, humanity has tried, in vain, to battle against impermanence. In the end, we all reach the same outcome, death. The Egyptians are probably the most famous society for their attempts to cheat death and achieve immortality. They built all those grand structures, in part, because they wanted to anchor themselves in life on this planet even stronger. They sought permanence. They wanted to live forever. There is an existential undertone of the fear of death that permeates much of the activity of our daily lives, whether we are consciously aware of it or not. One of the more common ways that it expresses itself is through attachment.

In our work, we build a lot of systems, products, and business processes. We are constantly building systems and programs, and developing products for our end users to use. We create things that go on and have lives of their own. Don't be fooled into having an unhealthy attachment to what you create; don't be attached to the systems you build, or to the products you create. You are not those products. Their demise is in no way connected to you. Their sun setting in no way indicates failure. In our field, in particular, change happens at lightning speed. Your work is going to become obsolete.

Every project you work on has a shelf life. Every product you create will eventually fall out of use. This is a good thing. ***You cannot remain relevant while remaining the same.*** By mastering the art of detachment, you will be better equipped to know when to retire your work and replace it with something better. You will know when that business process is outdated and in need of a replacement, and can proactively make the adjustments when the data dictates that that change is necessary.

Sometimes, the need for change may come sooner than anticipated. You must be aware of this at all times. You must loosen your grip and remain detached. We must be on alert for when something is in need of a refresh or removal. ***Constantly examine all that your department does and look for things that are no longer in line with the strategy of the office or no longer having the impact that they once had and pull the plug.***

I used to work with this extremely bright developer. He was a real data whiz. However, his attachment to his work was his downfall. Every time I met with him, he would quote me how many hours he spent on a project that ended up either not being used or going out of use. He let this eat him up inside. It got to the point that for about a year or two he let this feeling of attachment overtake him and it seemed to be all he could think about.

His attachment to his work took him down this really negative path. I wasn't the only one he would go on and on about this with. Whenever he had the chance, he would bring it up to whomever was around him; it got to the point that nobody wanted to be around him. The amount of time and energy that he spent in the negative grip of attachment to his work was astronomical. It blinded him from building better things that would have longer shelf lives and higher rates of usage.

If he invested a fraction of that time in learning what his end users wanted and why his systems fell out of use, he could have achieved greatness. It was sad to watch. He ended up getting relegated to a back office on another floor away from all of the end users. He was a really talented person, but because he was consumed by attachment, his impact was a fraction of a fraction of his potential.

Practice healthy detachment. Build something beautiful, realize it has a shelf life, and respect that. Even if it doesn't get used, who cares; you hopefully learned something in that process. Pick up and move on quickly. Be ready to walk away at any moment. You do want to build something that people use. You do want to build great products. You just don't want to cling to bad products or to the past. You always want to be looking and moving forward. Roll with the punches and master the art of healthy detachment.

Just because something doesn't get used for longer than a year or two does not mean that you built a bad product. The same is true even if it doesn't get used at all. You tried. As long as you learn from the process and don't constantly repeat the same mistakes over and over again, then this is ok. Never let failure weigh you down. ***Don't cling to old projects and old systems that are no longer of use.*** Release your attachment, let go of the project and move on to the next one. Who knows, the time may come back again for that project to attain relevance.

Earlier, we talked about plugging into your organizations DNA. When you do this, you are intimately aware of, and connected to, the changes that are happening at your organization in real time. When you get good at this, you can actually predict and anticipate future change based on direction and adapt for future change. Cultivating a healthy detachment from your work will make sure that you are making the appropriate adjustments at the right time, moving the irrelevant out of the way to make room for more impactful projects. A constant flow of fine-tuned work will spring forth and fill the needs of your organization.

Chapter 46

MALLEABLE

"The only thing I know, is that I know nothing at all."

Socrates
Plato's *Republic*

I love this quote from Plato's Republic. This was one of the central ideas of the Socratic worldview as outlined by Plato. What resonates with me about this quote the most is that if you engage the world from this vantage point, you tend to be malleable. You don't come to the table with strongly held biases or preconceived notions about what is and what is not true. ***You tend to be open to what the data indicates and you tend to not be threatened by other viewpoints.*** You tend to be open to working together with others to find solutions. ***You understand that through engaging others you are more likely to come to a better understanding of any given subject at hand.***

When conversing, are you malleable and open to the opinions of others, or are you hardened and closed off? Do you think you have superior knowledge or intelligence? Do you look down on your constituents because they may lack knowledge of systems and data? You might as well not engage with others if you can't open yourself up to others' viewpoints. Remember the importance of being able to engage in a dialectic with your constituents for solutioning and cultivating connection.

The second you think you know everything, you are essentially putting yourself in a self-imposed prison. Once in that prison, you are stagnating and not learning. You remove your power to change. If you know everything then you are perfect and there is no room for change. Change is life. Stagnation is death.

Make your best effort to remain open and malleable. Work alongside your constituents no matter how great or small their knowledge might seem when it comes to databases and data. You'll be surprised at how much insight and intelligence you can glean from their worldview.

I've noticed in my experience that some of my greatest insights came through engaging folks with little to no knowledge about the subject at hand. ***It is often through elementary questioning that overlooked opportunities come to light.*** The only way to recognize this is through remaining open to learning from anyone in any given situation that you may find yourself in.

Remain malleable. Remain alive. Don't stop asking why. Don't count anyone out. Don't overlook someone because you don't think they are a subject matter expert. Insight can come from anyone at any time. You must be open in order to be able to receive. You have to be malleable in order to be able to pivot and change when the time calls for change.

I get insight into problems that I am working on often in the strangest of places. I am constantly being changed by my encounters with the world It can happen when I hear the words of a passerby; when I'm listening to a song or watching tv or a movie; when I am ordering food; engaging in small talk with a friend or a stranger; cooking; cleaning; watching a commercial; reading an article; driving; observing nature; playing a game, etc. The possibilities are limitless. ***Insight knows no bounds. Insight does not discriminate and can utilize anything as a conduit for activation.***

Chapter 47

PIVOT

The Pivot is an essential tool to have in your Precision Prospect Development toolkit.

While working as a researcher at Stanford University, one of the geographic regions that I was assigned to was Silicon Valley. I had to become an expert in all things Silicon Valley. One of the most common terms I came across through conducting research and reading my periodical assignments was the term pivot. It seemed like every day there was an article about a startup or company pivoting in order to survive and thrive. I noticed that the companies that could master the art of the pivot were the ones that were successful and thriving.

What is a pivot? In the business world, a pivot is a term that refers to a conscious change in strategy or direction to achieve your company's vision. Pivots occur most often when the deployment of any given strategy does not lead to success. Variables are often uncovered in the process of deployment that point to new strategic directions that, if implemented, will achieve better outcomes.

The pivot is an essential tool to have in your *Precision Prospect Development* toolkit. You have to always be ready to pivot. You must remain malleable. You have to be ready to shift your priorities at any given moment. Don't cling to any current strategy or project. If you are too firmly planted in any given strategy, you won't be able to shift when the data demands a change in direction.

As your organization changes strategy, you must be ready to change your priorities to best meet the needs of the strategy. For example, leadership might say at one point in time, "We need new prospects. Go out there and find us as many major gift level prospects as possible." When this happens, you shift the focus of your team and put ratings front and center, and have the team go out and start rating people at an accelerated pace. Before you know it, the tide changes. Leadership comes back and says, "Wow. We have way too many prospects. More than we can ever get to. What we need now is more data on our current prospects so that we can engage them faster and with a higher degree of success." You then pivot again. You decrease emphasis on finding new prospects, and increase emphasis on finding and recording key data points on the current prospect pool.

The more you pivot, the more you learn. Past pivots can teach you a lot about what future pivots might look like. If you are plugged into the DNA of your office, you can use your knowledge of the current *zeitgeist*, combined with the knowledge of past pivots, to anticipate future pivots before they hit; you begin to make adjustments before senior leadership announces changing needs. The more in tune you are with the current *zeitgeist*, the more easily you can master the art of the pivot and fine tune your pivoting algorithm for successful course correction.

Plug into the DNA of your organization. Pay attention to the changing tides. Observe. Understand the unique variables of the *six elements* that underlie all things in your office. Remain open and malleable. Proactively pivot, shift strategy, and focus to meet the needs of your ever-changing and shifting office. Tweak your internal algorithms to achieve optimal success.

Chapter 48

THE EHTICAL HACKER

"To him that will, ways are not wanting."

George Herbert

Opportunity abounds. Windows of opportunity are constantly opening and closing all around us at every moment. But what happens if a window closes and you really need to get inside? You try to open it but nothing is working? What do you do then? Do you give up and move on? Wait? Try alternate strategies?

There are many paths you can take. Sometimes the right path is looking for the back door, or finding a hack that will cause the window to open back up. Hacking is a great tool to have and sometimes it is called for as the *next best action*. You should have at least one hacking algorithm that you use when you are doing your observation and analysis as described in previous chapters.

For me, the ethical hacker mindset is one that never gives up. It seeks out solutions on a level that is different than the more obvious. It looks for holes and openings that can be exploited to effect change. It looks for these little weaknesses or rules in the system (in our case, the DNA of the collective organization) that it can use to propel change. I added the word ethical in the beginning because when I speak of hacking I am talking about legal, authentic actions, that have integrity and compassion at their core.

In order to hack a system, you must have an intimate knowledge of that system. The process of plugging into the DNA of your office provides you with the foundational information you will need in order to become a DNA hacker. It can be argued that this entire book is a manual of sorts for hacking your system at work to enact positive change. As you learn more and more, you will see more and more areas that are ripe for hacking. For me this is a positive thing, and it does work. Just make sure that you are hacking in a way that does not harm others and is pushing for the collective good of everyone.

Save your hacking for those times when you know that you are onto something big but are not getting any traction by operating through the normal channels. Sometimes a colleague or manager may not be behaving ethically and setting up artificial roadblocks to prevent certain things from happening that they know are for the best of the organization but might not best serve their interests. Sometimes it may be just because it goes against their personal interests that they try to get in the way of positive progress.

When faced with this kind of a situation, your only option may be to hack the system to bring about this positive change for the betterment of everyone. This may require courage in addition to expert hacking skills. Make sure that you're keeping an eye out for balance when hacking and not setting into motion events that may end up harming you in a major way. It is good to stand up for what is right and use your hacking skills to ensure the right thing is done by everyone.

Chapter 49

POWER OF POSITIVITY

Positivity can turn the impossible into I'm possible.

One of the number one things that you can do to really make sure you have an impact at your organization is to incorporate as much positivity into your way of being as possible. ***A positive brain is 31% more productive than a negative one or one that is stressed out.*** 31% is huge. Imagine what you could do if you could increase your productivity by that much. Our outlook on life shapes in great detail our perceptions. Often we think that our perceptions are picking up what is out there and not realizing that they are filtered through our outlook prior to being perceived. ***Our outlook has a far greater impact on our lives than we may want to admit.***

I don't know about you, but I like working around people who maintain a positive outlook and smile. When I am in a meeting surrounded by other positive individuals, I tend to open up more, I get more creative; teamwork really thrives when basking in the sun of positivity. I have been in many meetings where the negative presence of just one individual threw off the entire meeting and little to nothing got accomplished.

The thing that I've noticed is that when you are always smiling, people want you around. If you can just shoot the breeze and talk about fun stuff, you build that rapport, you build that human connection; when you build that human connection, you have that bond, and then they feel more comfortable to have you around.

I am not always the best at maintaining a positive outlook or a positive presence. I enjoy existing in a positive state more than negative, and try my best to remain there and operate from that space, even when my experiences might not seem positive on the surface. Sometimes when I do express positivity, I get labelled a "Pollyanna". When I reflect further on this, I think that most are under the wrong impression about what it means to have positivity.

We don't really know what anyone else has gone through in their life or currently being subjected to, and the same goes for your life. Life is a narrow bridge and all kinds of things happen. It's very rare to walk through life unscathed; some people wear their scars on their sleeves and show them off; others hide them. Some wait until they build trust and know you to share their scars; others share them with anyone who will listen, and will reveal them in a first encounter. (Be very weary of those that share their scars too fast. Trust me on this. Those scars are often phantoms and the immediate sharing is a form of psychological manipulation.)

For me, realism is positivity. Many are confused and think that being a realist means calling it like it is in a negative way. That is not being a realist; that's being negative. Keeping it real is negativity in disguise meant to imprison you and prevent you from bringing forth your light and creativity and joy into this world. Don't fall victim to this mentality. There is actually no such thing as a truest objective viewpoint of reality anyway. There just isn't; there are too many variables. There is too much cause and effect for us to compute fully. So if you think your interpretation is the real and only true one, then you're sadly mistaken and you're doing yourself a disservice.

My brand of positivity was born out of the depths of despair. It comes from a place of deep dwelling and analysis and understanding of the world. It's not a Pollyanna complex. It's from an understanding of the illusions we are faced with, and the nonsensical super-fluctuating and ethereal existence of the things that cause us pain and strife. It comes from looking further ahead and understanding that what we are faced with currently isn't going to last. There is nothing anyone can do to me to bring me down, to stop me from existing in a state of love, to stop me from existing in a state of joy. No matter how hard they try. Realism - true realism is positivity. Allowing yourself to remain positive in the face of distraction is freedom.

Positivity is a choice. We can choose our outlook on life. Often we give our power over to others and then blame them when our choices end up in difficult situations. Don't forget that you have the power to choose your outlook. This is a freedom that is our birthright. Don't hand over your freedom to others.

With positivity as your main outlook you will attract good things into your life. Your relationships will improve. You'll feel less bothered by minor inconveniences. You'll be able to see the forest from the trees. You'll gain in confidence and eliminate fear. You'll experiment more. You'll move on from failure faster. You'll solve problems faster and with more elegant solutions. You'll enjoy your life more and increase your awareness of what goes on around you. Your intuition will strengthen. You'll activate and push into motion positive things all around you in ways that you cannot even imagine or understand and the collective ecosystem of your office, your networks, your friends, the earth and the universe will be forever grateful.

Chapter 50

MASTER THE FUNDAMENTALS

Simplicity = distilled complexity.

In other words, Simple + Simple + Simple = Complex

If simplicity is distilled complexity, then you can't build complex things without having a mastery of the simple. Let's repeat that. ***If simplicity is distilled complexity, then you can't build complex things without having a mastery of the simple.*** Mastering the fundamentals of your role is the only way that you are ever going to build great things. This is the only way that you are going to push the envelope and innovate. As we grow in our careers, we often neglect the fundamentals, viewing them as inferior, bucketing them into a lesser category with the belief that they require less skill to accomplish or that they are too basic to spend time working on. This couldn't be further from the truth. If you neglect the fundamentals of your role, if you ignore the simple tasks, you will limit the depth and breadth of your repertoire of ingredients that you can pull from to bake a complex solution. Your ability to create will be weakened.

Sometimes the foundational fundamentals of our roles are delegated to others as their core function, freeing up time for more complex work to be accomplished by more senior employees. This can create separation from you and an extra layer of foundational knowledge that you could utilize to push even further along with your more complex projects. Make sure that as you master the basics of your role, you are also mastering the foundational fundamentals of your role as well and revisiting them every so often to garner new insight.

I began my career in philanthropy as a gift processor at Stanford University. When I applied for the opening, I had no idea what the job was. I was an academic, a philosopher, who needed to obtain some job, any job, to pay the bills. I didn't really understand the business world at all. I didn't even really understand what the job was about. It was actually presented as a finance job on the accounting side. The title on the job card was "accounting assistant". It seemed like something I wanted to learn about, so I applied and accepted the offer.

As fate would have it, nine months later, I moved over to the Prospect Development team as an assistant director. I was a total newbie. I had little to no idea what this research job entailed or was all about either. What lured me was that I was told that I was going to be working with the GSB (Graduate School of Business), and was going to learn a lot about the business world, so I was all in as this was my biggest knowledge gap at the time.

What I discovered a few days into the job, was that my experience as a gift processor actually put me far ahead of the researchers who had been there for years and years because I had an expanded array of fundamental knowledge that they lacked. I had a deep knowledge of the details of our roles. They had to submit help desk tickets to get reports and to find things in the database. They didn't know all of the fields in the database, or how to harness the full power and potential of the database. A majority of the details of the database were foreign to them, whereas I could play the database like an instrument. Because I had been in gift processing and cross-trained in records management, I was a master of the fundamentals of our database. I wrote my own reports, I knew the structure of records. I knew where everything was located, and how to interact with it. I really tapped into these skills and combined them with the fundamentals of my research role, and this combination propelled me further than my manager expected.

This basic knowledge of the database that I had gained as a gift processor allowed me to open up entire new avenues as a prospect researcher. I was datamining the database to such great success that I was pushing out reports with prospects that were in need of major gift and principal gift ratings to other team members so that they could meet their monthly quotas. Six months into the role, I wrote my best datamining report ever. It was a pull that returned roughly 250 names out of a database of millions. Of those 250 names, I rated around 180 at the $250K and higher levels. Some folks on the team couldn't believe that I was accomplishing so much so quickly.

The difference between our work, was that I was harnessing this additional layer of simplicity. I was at all times connected to both the basics of the role, and thus able to connect multiple simplicities to produce creative, complex solutions. The rest of the team was doing great work as well, but they were hampered by this lack of fundamental knowledge. They were trapped at a higher level, cut off from the fundamentals, cut off from the simple, and thus were blinded by their elevated technical expertise.

Take a step back from your role. Re-read your job description. Try to take stock of the core, fundamental skills that your job requires. Do you have mastery of them? Is there an additional layer of fundamental skills that are beneath the basics of your role that you could benefit from learning? Does your job require working with certain software or databases? Do you have a fundamental knowledge of these tools? Take a look at what training is offered at your organization, and sign up for some classes that will expand your fundamental knowledge of the tools that your job requires you to use. I guarantee that you will learn things of great benefit from the intro class on your database, or an intro class on another software that you use.

I remember when I sat behind seasoned researchers at Stanford, shadowing their work so that I could learn how to do my job, I noticed a lack of a basic understanding of how to use the database. These were simple things like shortcut keys and basic search functionality. While they were simple, being able to incorporate them into our work was key to executing our function with minimal error. When I would say, "Oh by the way, did you know that if you hit the space bar after a search it runs an exact match?" Or, "If you hit F6, it takes you back to the home page." They would reply, "Oh cool, where did you learn that?" My answer was always the same, "The intro class." Even though they had taken the class once already, it had been years and years ago, and these fundamentals had become lost.

Remember that you are never too good to refresh your familiarity with the fundamentals. It is never too late to go back and take the intro class again. Do a periodic checkup to make sure that you have that fundamental knowledge to build from. Repeat intro courses every few years. Shadow the work of your colleagues so that you are knowledge sharing, especially when it comes to the fundamentals. Get cross-trained in the functions of others on your team so that you can expand your fundamental knowledge. Often the key to unlocking great solutions to the work problems we are trying to solve lies in the fundamentals of our roles, rather that some far off, exotic, super technical, expertise. Many (if not all) complex mathematical concepts and equations are rooted in simple arithmetic.

Chapter 51

BE A TOURIST IN YOUR OWN CITY

Embark on all undertakings as if you are a beginner.

Have you ever gone on a vacation where you learned and or did more in a foreign city within a week than you had done living in your own hometown for years? I am guilty of this for sure. There are cities I've been to for a weekend where I did more in two days than I've done in two years in my hometown. There is something about the seeming permanence of home that allows us to put off such things like visiting the local historic places of interest or tourist attractions. Why go do it this weekend, when we can literally go any weekend we want? It isn't going anywhere, and neither are we. Complacency sets in. Why go and see the local attraction when we live there, we already know what it's about, and don't need to actually visit like the tourists do. It's our city after all, right? It's ironic because people are constantly flying in from all over the entire planet just to see the local attractions that residents tend to take for granted. These tourists engage with our cities as explorers in ways we never do.

This same concept holds true as it pertains to our work. Once settled into a job, we tend to adopt a similar complacency as it pertains to our work. After some time on a job or in a role, we get comfortable with our skillset and the question of *why* dissipates from our lips and minds. We enter a state of knowing. Once in this state of knowing, we no longer have that curiosity to poke around because we falsely believe that there is nowhere else to poke around. The more knowledge we gain, the less we may feel the need to explore. After all, what is there to explore if we have already explored it all? ***The more we become experts, the less we explore.*** The more we settle into routine, the less we know about what lies beyond our everyday path.

Don't allow an increase in knowledge to decrease your curiosity. Try to increase curiosity with increased knowledge. ***The more you know, the more you should question.*** The more you learn, the more you should wonder what else there is out there to know. The more you learn, the more you should be inspired to try new things. The more something becomes familiar, the more you should look for the unfamiliar within the familiar.

The eye does not see what the mind does not know. This means that you will not see everything that *is* during the learning process. You may have gone up and down the same avenues before, but you were different then. There were things that didn't register before because you did not have the knowledge that would allow you to see them. You did not have the knowledge to unlock the visual. You didn't notice because there was nothing to register in your mind at the time. New knowledge unlocks new vision; new vision allows for more differentiation between what is. Every time you travel down a path, it doesn't matter how many times you have traveled down that path before, you are traveling from a different vantage point, because you are never the same person as you were the previous time you traveled that path. Even if you walk in the same footsteps as an earlier time, you are still walking from a different vantage point. Sometimes you will not notice anything different from one vantage point to the next; other times you will look at things on the path and wonder, "How did I not see this before? That surely was not there the last time I traveled down this path." This is because you couldn't see it; it was in a blind spot from your earlier vantage point. New knowledge created a new opportunity to notice what was once hidden. Be aware of this.

Because of this, it is important to adopt the beginner's mindset and be a tourist in your own city. ***If you operate from the false presupposition that knowing no longer requires growing, your input channels either become smaller or are closed off completely, preventing new information from entering into your mind.*** Be open to surprise. Understand that knowing leads to more growing, which leads to more knowing. The process does not end. The state of becoming does not stop until we are out of breath.

Remember the story about the new fundraiser from the chapter 40, "Constantly Refresh Your Data"? That story could just have easily been placed in this chapter as it outlines perfectly the success that happened to a fundraiser who approached their work with a beginner's mind. If that fundraiser did not approach their portfolio from a place of pure potential--from a beginner's mind--then they would have encountered the same roadblocks that the other fundraiser's encountered and not been able to unlock all of those gifts.

Never stop exploring. Human beings are natural explorers. It is a part of our DNA to grow and stretch and expand our horizons. With each new exploration, you will uncover something new. The more you learn and grow and change, the more often you should go back and travel down familiar paths. The more you travel down familiar paths with increased knowledge, the more you will see. The more you see, the more opportunities you will have to express your creativity and potential, and the more you will be able to build great things that can change your life, the lives of others, your organization, the world.

Chapter 52

SOLUTION ORIENTED VS. PROBLEM FOCUSED

Never orbit a problem.

Use the rocket boosters of positivity and creativity to propel you towards the solution.

Have you ever been around someone who always notices and points out problems? They seem to be able to spot an issue from a mile away and aren't afraid to engage in endless conversation about all that is wrong with their organization, department, manager, or just about anything that comes across their path. This is a bad habit, and it is not recommended that anyone engage in this kind of behavior. ***Don't allow yourself to get caught up in the gravitational pull of problems.*** Once you get sucked in, it is hard to get out. I've seen many talented people get consumed by the orbit of problems.

Have you ever been to a meeting where you are solutioning, and a team member will only want to talk about what won't work? Where the focus tends to be on how this won't work or that won't work. They say things like, "We tried that in the past, and it didn't work." "Oh no, have you seen our constituents? That's definitely not going to work." "You don't know Felicia like I do; this will not work." Sometimes you will even get a long, detailed history on the intricacies of how and why things don't work, almost as if it is a doctoral dissertation.

There is nothing that is less productive than this kind of attitude/mindset. I call it orbiting the problem. You will never find a solution if you are trapped in problem orbit. Because you are circling it, you can only see the problem; this is an even bigger problem if your goal is to find a solution. How can you expect to find a solution if you can only see the problem?

When you are solutioning, it is of vital importance to not allow yourself or your team to get sucked into the gravitational pull of a problem and get trapped in orbit, moving around and around the problem in circles. The problem should never exist as the center of your solutioning universe; when you find this happening, you must use the rocket boosters of positivity to break free from the gravitational pull of the problem, and thrust you out of orbit. Even if you have to drift a while in uncharted space while searching for a solution, that will always be better than orbiting the problem. And it will always be easier to set the course for a solution from this vantage point.

Try to cultivate a can-do attitude. All issues can be resolved. The resolution might not always be the most ideal, but a resolution can always be achieved. Be aware of the problem, but don't let that awareness blind you from your goal of finding a solution. Allow the problem to inspire action and creativity. Allow the limitations to push your limits of creativity and solutioning, not squash your creativity.

The only thing a problem should do is signal that something needs to change. It should not consume your focus. When solutioning, I like to approach it from an understanding of the problem and the elements involved. Examine it to pinpoint precisely where things go wrong and determine if a minor adjustment or repair is all that is required, or if an entire new solution is needed. Think about the end result that is desired and work backwards. If what is in place is no longer getting you your desired outcome, then what will? Iterate and don't feel pressure to get things right in the first version. As long as you are able to move the ball forward a little, you will get to where you need to be through further iteration. Sometimes we can't see the solution until we have first created a rough draft from which we are able to arrive at a new vantage point from which to see the solution.

Brainstorming sessions are invaluable. Set up a safe environment where you can be free to create. When brainstorming, examine all possible solution avenues. Walk down each avenue, and list out the strengths and weaknesses of each one. Remember, you only need to know so much about a problem in order to find a solution. ***The focus is on potential solutions, not pitfalls.***

The shortest distance from one point to another is a straight line. When solutioning, the path will almost never look like a straight line. It will zig and zag all over the place, and this is healthy. This means that you are iterating and looking for the best possible solution. When solutioning, the process of exploration is highly rewarding, and can uncover solutions and insights into other problems. Just make sure that when you are on your solutioning path, you don't get trapped in a repetitive cycle, like a figure 8. When you find that you are going around and around, you have to stop and get on another path. Rehashing old stuff will not move things forward, and your goal when solutioning is to move forward.

When you notice a problem, try to identify what element in the composition of the problem is the root cause of the problem. Think of how this can be tweaked so as to change the nature of the causal chain so that a different result occurs, one that will remove the problem from the system. Look at any and all problems like a puzzle or a game. Step back and remove your attachment to the process and envision how you can initiate a change that creates a solution. This will free your mind to engage in a playful manner and identify the most simple, elegant solution to almost any problem.

Problem creators and problem-centric employees are tough to be around. Often, problem focused people will socialize together and commiserate on all of the problems they are faced with. They do this because they feel powerless in the face of problems and need to find some validation of their worth through commiseration. This kind of bonding can forge strong friendships and relationships but they are toxic and such behavior is highly destructive and will only rob you of your power even more.

Try your best to steer clear of forging these types of bonds with others as it does not serve anyone involved. It will remove your ability to create and it will dull your ability to see solutions. More problems will crop up in your life because you are sharpening your ability to notice things that are inefficient or problematic. There is no perfection in existence so finding problems is really not a hard thing to do. Often problem finders will congratulate themselves for identifying problems and gossiping about them. Operate in this manner and your value as an employee will decrease, and, the next thing you know, your life will not have resulted in any art or creativity or beauty for the world. Are you spending your life in a manner that is allowing you to create positive solutions? Or are you creating a life that dulls you from positive expression and imprisons you in a dark, dank cell of negative problems? Do you really want to focus on negative things that irritate you so that you train your mind to only see these negative things thus creating a tortured existence for yourself?

The more you focus on solutions, the more you will sharpen your ability to spot solutions. Remember your brain is a muscle. ***All of these different tools that we are discussing in this book will grow in strength over time the more you use them.*** The more you strengthen your ***solutioning algorithm***, the more you will find that a solution immediately pops you're your head when you recognize a problem.

As this muscle grows in strength, you will find that you will become less bothered by problems and find more joy in offering solutions. You will actually see solutions so fast that you won't have time to be bothered by the problem. The only thing that will bother you will be not working to implement the solution. This will prompt you to take more ownership over the solutioning process and provide motivation to activate solutions and work harder with others to activate solutions instead of wasting time commiserating over problems over and over and over. (This will save you years of your life that would have otherwise been spent complaining about the same problems over. This way of existing can rob you of years of your life)

Once you have this realization and your mind switches over to this way of existing, you will be less disgruntled. You will increase your power and ability to exist in a state of freedom and be less bounded by self-imposed chains. ***The more you exercise the positive habits in this book, the more you will find yourself equipped with many highly helpful, sharp, functional, tools that can help you to be an extreme troubleshooter and MacGyver[18] yourself out of any situation free and clear and success.***

The more problems you solve, the more your services will be in demand. If you garner a reputation as a problem solver in your office, the next thing you know, you will be invited to more and more solutioning meetings and folks will open up to you more and more about problems that they are faced with in their work that is creating inefficiencies. Problem solvers are in high demand in an office setting. ***Folks with highly refined problem solving skills are indispensable.***

---

[18] One of my favorite television shows as a child, *MacGyver*, was a highly resourceful special agent who could use whatever objects were around him to escape out of even the deadliest of situations.

Chapter 53

THE DIALECTIC METHOD

The Dialectic Method should drive all interactions with constituents.

The *Dialectic Method* is a conversation between two or more individuals who seek to establish an understanding or truth about any matter at hand through a back and forth sharing of knowledge. The essential piece to the dialectic process involves a give and take. This process dates back thousands of years, and was a choice method of reasoning amongst philosophers and thinkers alike, in particular Socrates and Plato.

Our relationships with our constituents should always embody this ancient model of solutioning. Remember, our service model is rooted in cultivating positive connections and building relationships with our constituents. One way that really helps this process is approaching your work with your constituents from the Dialectic Method as a partnership; as a give and take, allowing everyone to have a voice.

We tend to say that we want to be partners with our constituents when it comes to us influencing them, but how many of us think of partnership when it comes to them influencing us? All of our work with our constituents needs to take place on a two way street. There should be little to no one-way communication. This is not the *didactic method.*[19] We are not telling them what to do, and they are not telling us what to do. We are entering into a partnership of engagement. Our solutioning should be the result of the blending of both of our expertise, not just the expertise coming from one particular side. We should all have a voice.

No one really enjoys being told what to do. People like to give their input. People feel good when they are let into the process of solutioning. We know this all too. I don't feel very good when I'm not invited to a strategy meeting or overlooked in an area where I know my opinion would have resulted in a better outcome.

As service providers, the bulk of our work involves others. We do not want to be order takers. If you are currently in the position of being treated like an order taker, take the advice in this book, and you will get out of that negative dynamic. Incorporating the dialectic method into your way of being will help to get you off of that one-way street and into a two-way partnership. We are partners; our value can only be realized to its fullest if the partnership dynamic is embedded deep into the culture of your collective organization.

If you are stuck on a one-way street pointing from your constituents to you, don't worry, you can change this. One way is to walk over to your constituents and engage in a conversation about some of their research requests to gather more information and insight. Another way is to write conversationally at the beginning of some of your more difficult research requests, explaining as if you were there talking in person. This creates the feeling like you are talking to them when they receive your communications.

---

[19] A one-way form of teaching/communication.

The dialectic method ensures that all voices are heard. It is important that your team be heard and your constituents be heard. As human beings we have a need to be seen and heard. This is a part of being social creatures. Fostering this ancient method of creating a collaborative environment will work wonders for your work and your team and your organization. This method has given birth to countless innovations for humankind.

Chapter 54

THE ITERATIVE PROCESS

Nature follows an iterative process.

A solutioning process that pairs nicely with the dialectic method is the iterative process. The iterative process is one were you put out a version of your product early on in the production phase, and get feedback from your constituents to see if you are on the right track. By receiving feedback at an earlier stage, you make sure that you don't invest time and effort in something that is not in alignment with your constituents. You are able to make refinements and keep the project on course. This shortens the time it would normally take to get to the end product, and, when you do get to the end product, you will have a higher chance of success because you included your constituents along the way to ensure that what you are building and working on is what they need.

A side benefit of the iterative process is that it allows your constituents to take more ownership over their requests. As they become more invested, they will learn more about the project. This increased knowledge will allow them to have a better grasp at the intricacies involved in the solutioning and they will begin to offer sharper guidance that will allow you to build a better solution that is more in line with what they want. Let's face it, one of the biggest obstacles that we encounter are stakeholders who don't know what they want but they know they need something.

I have been in this situation countless times. Through engaging our constituents in a dialectic process, we can fish out more of what they want in the beginning. Combine this with the iterative process and you are gold. Seeing the first iteration will open up their mind and cause them to have an ah-ha moment and provide you with better direction as to what they actually need. If instead of iterating, you take their initial guidance and spend months building something or working on something only to go back and have them react negatively to what you think is an amazing solution can be enough to break you. It can harm your relationship with your constituents and it can reduce your ability to create.

When this process of dialectic iteration is done well, it will forge a stronger partnership between you and your constituents and increase your value by getting you out of the role of order taker. As you work more closely together and ask for their opinions, it shows that you respect their opinion and that you have their best interest at heart. They will respect your way of solutioning and get a glimpse into the difficulty of our work and increase their respect for you and what you do. Rather than taking directions from a stakeholder and going off and spending hundreds of hours building what you think they need, you work in partnership and only spend time building what you know they need.

In addition to getting more solid feedback and having a more engaged stakeholder, this process can also strengthen your relationship with your constituents. Through inviting your constituents into the process in a more intimate level, you have the ability to forge a stronger bond. With a stronger bond in place, trust is increased. With increased trust, your conversations and solutioning can be more open and free. With more open and free communications, you can get to the root of issues faster and increase your ability to find the optimal solution.

Operating from a place of trust and safety will ensure that you are able to express your solutioning algorithm with as much experimentation and exploration gusto as possible. This will increase the elegance of your solutioning and your rate of solutioning success.

Don't worry about perfection or hold onto a project too long without soliciting feedback. Often we seek perfection and don't want to engage with our stakeholders until we have something that we deem to be the ideal state of what our constituent wants. Perfection is most often not the ultimate goal of any of the work that we do. Make sure you understand outcomes and deliver appropriate products that align with intent and outcome. Don't over deliver and don't under deliver. Iterate and engage with your constituents in a back and forth and the pressure for perfection will dissipate.

Without a solid, two-way, dialectic, partnership in place, your success rate will plummet. Without an engaged stakeholder, your solutioning has a lesser chance of being optimal, thus resulting in a sub-par product. Without an engaged stakeholder, your solutioning has a lesser chance of being utilized. Utilize the iterative process to build stronger relationships, deliver better results and increase your rate of success.

Chapter 55

THE EYE CANNOT SEE WHAT THE MIND DOES NOT KNOW

"It's not what you look at that matters, it's what you see."

Henry David Thoreau

In one sense, mind is all that exists. The power of our minds goes far beyond anything anyone can imagine. Our thoughts and our beliefs are responsible for creating our realities in a way we may never understand. Not only do they create our realities, but they also act as the filter through which we interpret reality. In that sense, the word *reality* loses some of its meaning because it doesn't really exist outside of us as this purely objective thing.

Philosophers have been grappling with this issue since the beginning of civilization. Our minds are like experience magnets; they draw in experiences based on our beliefs and focus. We sometimes ask ourselves, "Why is this happening to me, "never coming to a realization of why, but the answer will most likely be tied to something concerning our beliefs.

There is an additional layer of complexity to the issue of reality versus mind. We are often not even reacting to a complete picture of reality because of shortcuts that our minds take in interpreting reality. In an effort to conserve energy and move faster, our minds take perception shortcuts.

For example, if there is an apple in front of you, and you have a familiarity with apples, your mind will actually create an image of an apple for you faster than you can examine the actual apple that is in front of you. At first glance, your mind does not think that it is wise to expend the extra energy that it takes to collect and process data down to the grainy details so that you can know this apple's tiniest of blemishes. So the mind programs over the apple in front of you, an image of an apple of similar shape and size to make it easier for you to know what is there, and to take up less energy in the process.

This is actually precision at its finest. If you are then interested in possibly eating the apple, you might look at it further. At this point, you begin to interact with the apple in front of you more and are in need of a more accurate representation of the actual apple in front of you. You look more closely and your mind does not take the large shortcuts, but allows you to expend the energy to examine in more detail the apple in front of you.

Suddenly you notice a big bruise on the side. The more you look at it, the more the bruise stands out. You wonder why you didn't notice the bruise before because now it is all that you see. This is because the bruise was not there before. You were not interacting 100% with this apple. You were interacting with likely 5% of that apple and 95% of what your past experiences of apples.

I learned that the eye cannot see what the mind does not know in elementary school after being introduced to the infamous bus activity called the "punch-bug" game. Many of you may remember this game from your childhood. For those who don't, I will explain further. I attended Hunter Elementary school in Raleigh, North Carolina. Hunter is what they call a magnet school. It brings in children from all backgrounds and all areas surrounding a given location in order to ensure a diverse body of students.

What this meant for me was an hour bus ride in the morning, and again in the evening. Being cooped up on that bus for so long at such a young age, I was constantly getting involved in shenanigans and getting in trouble. (In fact, I almost got kicked off at one point, but that is neither here nor there.) One of the games we played to keep ourselves occupied on the bus was called the punch bug game.

The rules of the game were simple. Whenever a VW Beetle passed by, the first to yell out "punch-bug" got to pick one person from whoever else was playing, and punch them as hard as they could on the arm or leg. Not the face. (Hey, we had some civility, ha-ha.)

I still remember when the older kids were explaining the rules, my first and only objection was not that I was going to be getting potentially pummeled by kids three grades older than me, and that I didn't stand a chance of surviving, but instead I complained that those cars are too rare on the road and that no one will ever get to punch anyone because we will be lucky if we see one a week let alone one a day. I said "I never see those cars. This game won't be any fun." The older kids patted me on the head and said, "Oh, don't worry about that, you'll see."

As soon as we began playing the game, it was like all of a sudden these cars came out of the woodwork. There were punch-bugs everywhere. We were slugging each other left and right. What I realized after a few days of playing that game was that it wasn't that these cars didn't exist on the roads before, it was just that my mind wasn't looking for them, so I didn't see them before. Now that they are on my radar, I am noticing them more and more. My reality shifted, and these cars seemingly dominated the roads.

There is so much that exists in the cosmos that we are oblivious to. We don't even know what is happening within our own bodies. When applied to our work, we must be aware that we have blind spots; our blind spots are due to our limited vantage point. Just because we may not see a solution in the current environment does not mean that a solution does not exist. Keep your imagination open. Remain malleable. You are always operating from a place of limited knowledge, based on limited data, and limited variables combined with a mind that takes perceptual shortcuts. We draw our best conclusions from what we have available to us at any given time. The more we learn, the more we can see.

The more we are aware of our perceptual shortcuts, the more we will be able to know when to expend that extra energy that seeing clearly requires. The more we will know when to stop, pause and focus in and change our vision from 5% reality, 95% mind, to 95% reality, 5% mind. This means that what you previously viewed will need to be looked at again and again and again. This means that you will need to slow down and pause, taking in each new view coming from a new vantage point, unlocking new knowledge, causing increased vision.

This means that you will not see everything that *is* during the learning process. You may have gone up and down the same avenues before, but you were different then. There were things that didn't register before because you did not have the knowledge that would allow for you to see them. You did not have the knowledge to unlock the visual. You didn't notice because there was nothing to register in your mind at the time. New knowledge unlocks new vision, new vision allows for more differentiation between what is.

Every time you travel down a path (it doesn't matter how many times you have traveled down that path before), you are traveling from a different vantage point, because you are never the same person as you were the previous time you traveled that path. Even if you walk in the same footsteps from an earlier time, you are still walking from a different vantage point. Sometimes you will not notice anything different from one vantage point to the next, other times you will look at things on the path and wonder, "How did I not see this before? That surely was not there the last time I traveled down this path." This is because you couldn't see it because it was in a blind spot from your earlier vantage point. New knowledge created a new opportunity to notice what was once hidden. Be aware of this.

Awareness of this is key. This is another important tool to have in your *Precision Prospect Development* toolkit. The more you can master a true understanding of the *six elements* of any given situation, the more precise you can set your course. The more you are able to see when examining the six variables, the more precise you can be. The more you know, the more you must travel down familiar paths, picking up additional knowledge that you were not able to see and/or carry on previous trips. Understand when you need to pause and focus and engage more closely with the reality that is in front of you, versus when you can conserve energy and move on with a majority mind driven matrix.

Chapter 56

THE IMPORTANCE OF CREATIVITY

Let go of everything. Free your mind from compartmentalization. Engage in the present moment, and allow your thoughts to freely create whatever combinations they see fit.

A long time ago, when Netflix was a DVD subscription company, they almost went out of business due to the high cost of running their warehouses. The costs were high because every time a DVD was returned through the mail, they would meticulously file it away in its proper place, on a shelf, according to whatever arranging system they had in place. The cost of maintaining order was so high, that it was bankrupting them. In order to survive, they needed to find a more cost-effective way to run their warehouses. The warehouse experts couldn't think of a better way to do things.

The company brought in non-warehouse experts and had them look to see if they could think of a more efficient way to operate. The non-warehouse experts looked at the operation and were puzzled at the arrangement of things. They were curious as to why they spent so much time putting the DVDs back in their proper order when they are pulled so quickly and sent back out again. Through their insights, Netflix adopted a new way of processing their incoming and outgoing mail. They threw away the concept of arranging their DVDs on a shelf in a certain order, and instead kept them in baskets and continuously ran them through a conveyer belt, scanning each one at least once a day. If it was ordered by a customer, then it would get routed to outbound mail; if no one had asked for it, it would go back in the bin to be scanned again the next day. This new process cut down their costs and sped up their ability to get DVDs to their consumers.

This story is a great analogy of the power of creativity. Think of the warehouse as your mind. Think of the DVDs as your thoughts. We often try too much to compartmentalize our thoughts, and this prevents creativity to flow freely.

If I had to think of what makes me most happy about being alive, I would say that it is my ability to create through unbounded self-expression. I am at my best when I am let loose on a problem, issue, or topic, and be allowed to just do whatever I want. Some of my best work has come from being able to do this.

My previous manager at Stanford, Linda Collier, teased me once and said, "Nathan, I don't know how you do it. I give you a problem to solve. You take notes, smile and tell me you will get back to me. You disappear into your office or wherever you go and you come back, and somehow you present me with this elegant solution."

I was able to do this for her, in large part, because she gave me the freedom to create. She allowed me to go through the creative process on my terms and gave me the space I needed to give birth to the solution. I owe her a debt of gratitude for this because I wasn't afraid to leave the office for an hour or two if I needed to go find inspiration while I worked on a problem. Because I had no fear and knew that she trusted me, my ability to produce increased exponentially. This production ensured that my work was successful. Had she had a tighter rein on me and scolded me for behavior that was conducive to my creativity I wouldn't have been successful in the role.

Get to know yourself and what type of setting you thrive in creatively. ***Are you currently in a position that is nurturing your creativity?*** If not, what can you change to ensure you are able to be your best and create elegant solutions for your constituents? Make the necessary changes so that you are able to operate in your creative space as often as you need to enhance your productivity. It is vital that the conditions be right so that you are able to express your genius.

I experience creativity as the outpouring of content from within that is a mix of the unconscious and conscious mind. It works like an algorithm, a creativity algorithm. I can feel the constant combinations being put together in the background of my brain, as if I am trying to crack the safe of my own mind. Once a combination hits and is deemed worthy of creation, it hits my consciousness, and I have to run an analysis to either give it the green light for actualization, or hang on to it until it comes back, if it ever comes back. I carry around a little book and write ideas down when they come to me as much as I can because, if I don't get it out when that inspiration of creativity strikes, it might not come back.

When I go through and read the notebook, I sometimes look at it and wonder; *who wrote this?* When this happens, I'm always so happy that I wrote that down because if I didn't it would be lost and it might not ever come back to me. Or if it does come back it might not be the same or as good as when the inspiration struck. When creativity strikes, make sure you take action on it in as timely a manner as possible. Sometimes you are the only conduit for something to come into being, and if you ignore that moment, it may never come back again.

Get a notebook for yourself for your creative ideas (or use the notes on your phone) so that you can always be prepared to create when the mood strikes. I find that I can get something done much faster if I am in inspiration mode than not. If I wait and don't listen to my intuition and act when the creative moment strikes, it is always much harder to produce. It will take a lot longer to get it done and the final product won't have that same feel or level of beauty that it otherwise would have had if I had done it in the moment of inspiration.

Creativity is one of the most important of the foundational attributes for successfully operating at the highest level and implementing a successful P*recision Prospect Development* program. As you observe, analyze and implement the ability with which you are able to harness creativity to navigate the more successful you will be. The attribute of creativity is the perfect pairing with

We spoke about the importance of having an open mind so as to be able to fully understand what is going on around you and to be able to make the best decisions. Being open is key for enhancing your creative process. As alluded to a few paragraphs above, for me, the creative process works a lot like analytics. It's an algorithm. My creativity algorithm is set to be as open as possible to everything that is out there in existence and to not reject anything based on a closed-off belief system that filters out potentially valid possibilities. The creativity algorithm is intimately tied to all other algorithms and their output and even searches them for inspiration. **The less boundaries you place on your creativity algorithm the more creative you can be.**

As we move about the office and interact with different folks and engage in a dialectic (give and take) with them we are exposed to their worldview and their personal algorithms. They speak from their constructs and you speak from yours. This is like a dance. When someone speaks to you through their constructs make sure that you don't lose sight of yours and that you don't get forced into viewing the world with the boundaries that their expressions build. Creativity is the way that you can ensure that you are able to break free from the boundaries of their worldview and engage in the dialectic that is authentic to yourself.

Multiple times throughout the years, I have found myself having that dreaded conversation with my managers on the subject of promotion and it would almost always go something like this: I had been working really hard and was successful in everything I was doing. I was doing the job of someone a few levels above me but still stuck in a lesser role. This was inhibiting my ability to get my work done effectively due to the hierarchal constructs titles create. My role had expanded naturally but my title was behind the times. In our discussion, I was posed a question: "What motivates you: title or money?" I took a second and paused. With a puzzled look on my face I answered back, "Well both are important, yes, but I'm not really wired to think that way. I can't choose one of those two. From my view my role and responsibilities have expanded and this is more about a need that the organization has that needs to be filled. The current structure that I am in is not reflecting the reality of the situation. While of course having a better title is better and more money is always going to be welcomed those are not the motivating factors." It took me a little bit to get to that answer. I wasn't as eloquent as I could have been and didn't make as strong of a case as I would have if I didn't get a little stuck in that narrow framework that was thrust upon me in the heat of the moment where we were discussing something that was really important. The outcome of which could have a big impact on my life.

I have been in situations like this countless times and for the vast majority of my life I would allow the question to box me in and not speak my truth because I allowed the interaction with another worldview to temporarily cloud mine so that I thought it was mine and would operate within those confines and give an answer that wasn't even in the realm of how I think. Through building out my confidence in myself, sharpening my skills as an observer and practicing detachment, I have gotten better and better at understanding when I am in one of those situations and allowing my creativity to help me break free from the confines of the limitations of others and operate from my own worldview.

Another example of how we can be boxed in by a limited view or the presentation of reality as if there are only a set number of listed options is the age old question of looking at a glass of water and being asked is it half full or half empty. Our answer is supposed to be informative on how someone views the world and if they are a pessimist or an optimist. A friend of mine recently sent me a clever meme that reimagined the possible answers to this question by adding a third option: the glass is perfectly balanced. I enjoyed reading that meme because it broke from the mold of two options and posed a clever third that is equally as valid as the other two. When questions are posed in a way of giving options it creates this illusion that the options presented are all that exists.

There were two quotes in Chapter 38 that combined together can shed some light into creativity. In the words of Abraham Joshua Heschel, "**The meaning of life is to build life as if it were a work of art.** You're not a machine. When you're young start working on this great work of art called your own existence... Remember the importance of self-discipline… Study the great sources of wisdom... Remember that ***life is a celebration***… ***what's really important is life as celebration***." Combine this with what Aristotle says about art: "The aim of art is to represent, not the outward appearance of things, but their inward significance." Blend this data together and there is a valuable insight.

Human beings are inward facing beings. Our ability to go deep within is sacred and it is this ability that allows us to actualize our creativity. If the meaning of life is to live as if your life were a work of art and art is the outward expression of our inward significance, then then meaning of life is to live a life of the creative expression of our inner significance. ***Celebrate your creativity and your creative achievements and celebrate the creative achievement of others.***

This book is a creative expression of my inward significance. I know that it is not written in a traditional manner and is likely filled with faux pas, but nevertheless I want to try to offer up what I have learned throughout my life to try to help propel others to find their own form of success and unleash their voice and creativity on the world in as unbounded of fashion as possible.

Combine all of the ideas from this book and pair them with creativity. Work on opening up your creativity algorithm so that you can flourish and implement sustainable solutions in complex situations. Utilize your creativity algorithm for every output you have to achieve optimal results. Whenever you feel like you are being boxed in by limitations don't panic or let fear take over. Simply breathe and turn on your creativity algorithm to look for an escape hatch or a way to break free from illusory limitations.

Chapter 57

LESS IS MORE

The more information that we are faced with, the less we see.

Less is more is one of the foundational operating principles that I work from. Try your best to never over complicate your work. If a constituent asks for a skateboard, give them a skateboard. Don't build them a hover-board and, upon delivery, overwhelm them with new information about why the hover-board is superior to the skateboard. If you do this, not only will they not have their skateboard, but they likely will not use the hover-board either.

Make sure you are always building and delivering what is asked for. No more, no less. They will come to their own realization that the product is inadequate if it is indeed inadequate. At that time, they may request something different. At that time, you might want to show off the extended capabilities of something more advanced.

I was watching a show on kid artists once, and a teacher said something I will never forget. She said most art from children can rival any master, the key is knowing when to take it away from them so that they don't keep adding until it no longer retains its artistic merit. Think of your work like this. Know when to stop. Try to understand where that edge lies with your own work. Do your best to pull back and not cross that edge of over complication.

Use your distillation powers to distill your own work down to the core essential parts that will have the greatest impact. Remember Professor Polen's advice, you want to deliver a jar of maple syrup, not gallons of sap. Go over your emails and remove unnecessary words. Get to the point as fast and with as little wording as possible. This will increase the chance of success by increasing the likelihood that folks are going to read and comprehend your output.

Master this concept, and more of your work will achieve the desired impact. More of your work will make it to your constituents and receive the attention it deserves. Balance this with all of the other lessons in this book, and you will be unstoppable. Less is more.

Chapter 58

QUESTION EVERYTHING

Never accept anything at face value.

The pace at which things change will vary greatly from thing to thing. Sometimes things can change fast; other times they can change slowly. The variable rate at which change occurs is hard to predict. And the speed can go from fast to slow in an instant and then back again.

Our ability to observe, collect data and analyze are key for our success. In order to be highly skilled observers, we have to sharpen our ability to ask questions. The best observers actively question during the observation process from a detached, non-judgmental position. Asking the right questions will unlock important data that you will need to garner from your observations to inform your analytics.

Question everything at all times, in every way, as much as is necessary to take the next best action. Asking the right questions can uncover changes you were not aware of. ***Sometimes it is by asking the right question, at the right time, in the right way that unlocks the answer.***

If you maintain a healthy questioning of everything, even down to your assumptions, you will be in a much better position to deliver the right *actionable intelligence* at the right time. You will know how to best distill your data down to the right flavor of syrup so that it tastes sweet to your fundraisers and have them coming back for more.

Allow the *six elements (Who, What, When, Where, Why, How)* to drive your questioning. Going through each one for everything you encounter will ensure that you are engaging in a thorough enough analysis. Keep these elements on your mind for everything.

Think about the *six elements* from at least three angles:

1. What is the current state?

2. What is the ideal state?

3. What are other possible states?

Your answers will help you to answer the next question which is: What, if any, action do I need to take? Allow this way of operating to guide you in your work and inform you in how to proceed, arrange projects and invest your time and energy.

Chapter 59

SYNERGY

Synergy lies at the intersection of interconnection.

As our society advances, the need to do more with less increases exponentially. As our organizations grow, the majority of the burden of doing more with less often falls at the feet of Prospect Development. The added pressure caused by the need to do more with less can cause much stress and affect our work in a negative way. Practicing *Precision Prospect Development* offsets this pressure in myriad of ways.

One of the most effective and immediate ways to do more with less, is to identify and harness areas of synergy. Harnessing synergy means to harness the interconnected nature of existence. Synergy lies at the intersections of interconnection. Look for these intersections in your workflow, on your team, in your office. Once identified, set up business process flows that make use of the synergies.

Examine all of your team's business processes and the business processes of other teams that affect your workflow. Can you find areas of improvement based on synergies? Are there any tweaks or changes that can be made so that there is no repetition of work throughout each process? Examine your department structure. Does the current structure allow for work to be streamlined? Does it allow for you to take full advantage of natural synergies that exist?

The current structure of my team at the City of Hope is highly conducive to synergy. Prospect Development at City of Hope is made up of six units: Prospect Research, Prospect Management, Business Intelligence, Business Analysts, Records Management and Training. We are essentially Prospect Research + Development Services + IT – Gift Processing – Database Hosting and Support. Since we all roll up into one unit, our ability to harness synergy is amazing. The key is having a strong vision, expressing that vision, and getting all teams to act in concert with each other while implementing the vision.

Our business analysts ensure that our constituents have the appropriate systems in place to support their business needs. When they build out a new system, it often requires some sort of training to take place so that the system can take root and be utilized by the team for which it was built. This is where our trainer comes in and builds out training materials based on specs and inserts the new process into the training curriculum.

The Business Intelligence team takes the new system and builds out a suite of dashboards and automations to ensure for the most efficient and informative workflow. The prospect management and research teams act as consultants with the business analysts in order to make sure that it is in alignment with other systems. Our records team looks out for prospects as they work maintain the health of the database; as they come across leads, they send those to the prospect research team to be researched and rated and put into the queue to be assigned by prospect management.

All teams work in concert with each other and share knowledge of current happenings, so as to operationalize and streamline as much business processes as possible. We have monthly meetings where we go over the vision of the department and look for areas of synergy that we can incorporate into our workflows.

Don't just look for areas of synergy within your team. Look for areas of synergy outside of your team. Harness synergy whenever and wherever possible. Prospect Development works with almost all, if not all, of the other departments within the organization. A natural outcome is to recognize areas of synergy that others can't see. Call them out and get the ball rolling so that the synergies can be utilized.

Actively engage your work looking for areas of synergy. Set your internal algorithms to search for synergy patterns so that you can do more with less. The sharper your synergy algorithm, the more you will be able to identify areas where you can save yourself time and effort through sharing and collaboration with others. As with most of the other advice in this book, engaging in your work in this manner will set you on course for success and will strengthen all of the other areas of your work life so that you are operating in balance with the collective, plugged into the DNA of your office and activating positive output beyond measure.

Chapter 60

LEARN FROM EVERYTHING, EVERYONE

"Early morning sunshine, tell me all I need to know."

The Allman Brothers Band

Become an expert in anything and everything that comes across to your desk. Whenever you are in a meeting and somebody has a question that no one can answer or something is discussed and you don't know the answer, don't settle for ignorance. Instead take notes on the topic during the meeting and afterwards do some research and educate yourself on that topic. This is a great way to prioritize how you should go about filling out your knowledge gaps.

If a topic surfaces once, it's likely to surface again and you don't want to be in the dark about it when it comes up the second time around. As you do this more and more, it will help you to become an expert in many areas where there is a need for an expert. Due to the lack of others in your office who understand the topic, your opinion will soon be sought out by key stakeholders.

Systematically take stock of all that you are responsible for doing in your role. When you have this, look at what kinds of knowledge and skills you will need to have in order to be the very best in your current role. Think about your career and your future. Think about where you would like to be in your next phase. Ask yourself, "Do I have the knowledge and skills required to take this next step? If not, what do I need to learn in order to be prepared so that I can successfully make the transition?"

While working for Stanford, I became an expert in queries. This wasn't an assignment given to me by my manager. Becoming an expert in queries wasn't something that I was supposed to do or something that I was supposed to know, but it helped me to do my job so much better. The fundraisers that I was working with had a lot of needs that required me to combine my datamining expertise with the ability to generate my own lists from the reporting side of the database. This meant queries. I recognized that and proactively went about filling out my knowledge gap so that I could be a more productive employee. After taking a few trainings, and, with some practice, I was able to write my own queries, instead of waiting a week for someone else to write them for me. This ability made me so much more valuable to my constituents because they had a lot of needs that revolved around getting access to various lists of prospects.

Don't limit yourself. Learn as much as you can about everything that comes across your desk day to day, especially topics concerning philanthropy. Learn as much as you can about fundraising. Learn as much as you can about what it's like to be a frontline fundraiser. Learn about your local markets. If you are in LA, be an expert in the entertainment industry and the music industry. Learn about the top companies that are around you so when it comes up in meetings you can talk about it. You can throw out a few facts that can help move the conversation along. Learn about the top companies that are around you so when it comes up in meetings you can talk about it. You can throw out a few facts that can help move the conversation along and inform strategy.

Know key facts about your organization and your office. Know who your Board of Directors are, know who your key volunteers are, know who your top prospects are, as those names are constantly going to be coming up in meetings and the more you know about them, the more familiar you are with them, the more valuable you will be in those meetings. Understand what counts in your organization most. Also, understand the goals of your organization, the goals of the different folks that you support, and then direct all your projects to those goals.

Know as much as you can about finance. The more you can learn about finance and real estate the more successful you will be in this field. Take some classes, go to lectures, read Wikipedia, do whatever you have to do to learn finance. Learn about venture capital, private equity, investment banking, hedge funds, IPOs, insider stock, indirect vs. direct stock, etc. The more you know in this area, the easier it will be for you to identify prospects and accurately calculate their net worth for your research ratings.

Understand your constituents. Know as much as you can about your fundraisers; take them out to lunch, hang out with them, don't be afraid. We should all be like Johnny 5 from *Short Circuit*, enthusiastically gathering input wherever we can find it to inform us as to the nature of the casual chain of existence.

There's data everywhere. Open up and soak it all in. Run it through your multiple algorithms for optimal output. Allow experience to be your teacher, but don't *just* allow your experiences to be your teacher; allow the experiences of others to teach you as well. Learn from both your past successes and mistakes as well and the past successes and mistakes of others.

As you observe and learn about the *six elements* of all aspects of your office, make sure that you are learning lessons. You will notice many instances of 'if this, then that.' Incorporate this knowledge into your experimentations to see how repeatable past success can be and learn about the intricacies of the interplay of the six variables on outcome and how slight tweaks to any variation of any variable can lead to different outcomes.

Chapter 61

TEAMWORK

"Two are better than one only if two act as one"

Coach Mike Krzyzewski
Duke Basketball

I grew up in a lot of different places on the east coast, but for about seven years during elementary, and part of middle school, I lived in Raleigh, North Carolina. When I was in elementary school, I attended Duke Basketball camp in the summer. It was a two week program where you lived in the Duke dorms and played basketball. Coach Mike Krzyzewski led the camp and every day I attended a few classes taught by coach K himself!

Looking back on that experience, I can't believe it happened. The experience was amazing. It really taught me the importance of teamwork. Every day, Coach K talked about the importance of teamwork, and had us do drills that built trust between team members and emphasized working together as a cohesive unit rather than showboating and hogging the ball. We learned how to harness the power of each other to form a super unit where the collective is stronger than any individual. Through engaging in healthy teamwork, synergy activates and gives everyone on the team an extra boost of whatever it is that they may need to thrive.

Human beings are social creatures. Prospect Development is in the connection business. As we create connections, we forge bonds. Our bonds are teams. We must always work together with those around us if we are to achieve success. Working together extends our power and our reach and allows us to see further ahead so that we can adjust our course for success.

Precision Prospect Development is a team sport. It requires the ability to harness synergy. This is not about elevating yourself, your ego, or moving your way up to the top to gain personal power. That way of existing will never serve you, your organization, or those around you. But don't confuse expressing your genius with being selfish. Sometimes jealous individuals will try to make you think that expressing your genius is a selfish endeavor. Don't fall for this trap.

Enjoy the fruits of your labor, and spread your knowledge to those around you. Express yourself and create. This entire book is about empowerment. Historically, as an industry, we have not had a voice. We have not had a seat at the table. We have to push to make this happen if our organizations are to thrive. The ecosystem we are plugging into needs us to have a voice at the leadership table for the survival of the collective organism that is your organization.

The strong have strength to build up the weak, not to break them. The smart have wisdom to educate the unwise, not to trick them. The wealthy have riches to help the poor, not to control them. Those with food have food to help those with food insecurity. The list goes on and on. In the context of teamwork, this means take your skills and toss them into the collective to benefit the entire organization.

Work with your team, not against it. Look for areas of collaboration. I am very careful when I invite folks to meetings and tend to err on the side of inclusivity. It is important that when assembling a team, you know the strengths and weaknesses of your group so that you can pick the right colleagues for each meeting to create the synergy to produce the best output. It is important to have the right number attend. Too many, or too few, and you won't have the same output. Use the *six elements* to help you assemble teams for optimal output.

When you plug into the DNA of your organization, you are also plugging into the DNA of your team, as your team is a part of your organization. It may be helpful to have a separate focus and strategy for your team and for teamwork in general. High functioning teams operate as one. They look to each other for support and build each other up instead of tearing each other down.

I tell my team that they need not fear "the bus" because I am not looking for them under a bus. I don't want their interactions with each other be based on the fear of being thrown under the bus. I don't want that to stop collaboration and teamwork so I say "I'm not looking under the bus. I am alongside you with my sights set on the goal line and will do what I can to ensure that we successfully meet goal and/or exceed goal. Work together as a team. Work out issues in a safe environment but keep in mind that the goal is important for the success of the entire team and the only way to get there is to work together."

(I try my best myself to not be afraid of being thrown under the bus by others. I have gotten to a point where I don't really even notice it when it happens or if it does happen I notice it and I don't allow it to create a reaction in me. I simply look to see if there is any validity to the critique and, if there is, make the necessary adjustments to myself so that in the future I don't have that weakness. I don't draw any more attention to it than I have to and move on. I try to let me work speak for itself and show up every day with integrity and goodwill towards others. This allows me to have the confidence to move forward without fearing potential damage from an unruly colleague who takes jabs through highlighting possible flaws in front of others.)

Without this fear of being punished for minor quirks like tone in email, improper cc'ing of managers, etc. you can focus on the goal and get there successfully. We all know that things may happen along the way and issues can arise while working on projects but if we stick together and operate as one unit we will always arrive on time.

Most of the chapters in this book deal with aspects of how to operate in a teamwork style for ultimate success. If you follow the advice in these pages you will be able to navigate the waters of your team and organization and create relationships and dynamics that are conducive to building tightly knit teams.

Chapter 62

EVERYONE IS A PROSPECTOR

"I want to live, I want to give. I've been a miner for a heart of Gold"

Neil Young
Heart of Gold

Just as we are all fundraisers, we are also all prospectors. Due to the high level of importance that dollars in the door plays in the value chain, finding viable prospects to match with programmatic pathways will always be a top priority. Of all the work that we do, prospecting ranks in the top in terms of value. Thinking like a prospector is a key part of enacting *Precision Prospect Development* and is one of your key motivational ideals that you need to cultivate and spread across the psyche of your team and organization. This should be on everyone's minds at all times as they engage in their unique roles.

Just as important as it is to cultivate the idea that everyone is a fundraiser, so is it equally important to cultivate the culture that everyone is a prospector. This is most true for all members of the greater Prospect Development team, especially if it is not in their job description. It is important to cultivate and promote that mindset amongst the team, and within yourself, that you are always a prospector.

A unifying goal for your department or team is to ultimately find prospects that your organization can run through the solicitation cycle and ask for gifts. With this as one of your overarching goals, everyone's directive should be to operate within their core responsibilities in a way that will bring in more and better prospects.

For example, thinking like a prospector for an individual on a records management team could translate into the following: A request is received to update an address from someone in the annual fund for a prospect. As they are update the address they notice that the prospect lives in an affluent area. They look and see that the prospect does not have a research rating. They then run a quick Zillow search of the property and see that it was purchased for $4M six months earlier. They then send the name off to the research team for a rating and potential assignment.

Implementing the idea that everyone is a prospector will have tremendous impact on your Prospect Development shop; it will widen the net and the number of team members who are out fishing for prospects. This will increase the number of positive prospects identified in less time and with less resources, taking advantage of the natural synergy that exists amongst the teams that deal with data. Our team at City of Hope operates in this manner and we have been able to increase our ability to catch top prospects.

Earlier, when we spoke about our impact on the bottom line, we demonstrated that we impact the bottom line in two major ways: our ability to create portfolios through prospecting to expand the fundraiser count and our ability to increase the amount of revenue generated by each fundraiser we support. Make sure you always keep prospecting as a top priority and are highly in tune with the need for more and better prospects for your current fundraisers and for fundraisers who have not yet joined your organization.

Chapter 63

THE IMPORTANCE OF FAILURE

"Tis a lesson you should heed, try, try again.
If at first you don't succeed, try, try again."

Thomas H. Palmer

Failure is often the conduit for the activation of greatness. Because of this, we must embrace failure. So much can be learned or set into motion through actions that result in setbacks, roadblocks or failures. If we fear failure and avoid it at all costs, we could set into motion events that lead to giant breakthroughs. Experimentation and iteration will never achieve 100% success and if they do then you are not pushing the boundaries enough.

Our Chief Philanthropy Officer at City of Hope often says to the fundraisers that if they have too high of a success rate of asks to gifts then we are either waiting too long to ask, not asking for enough or not asking enough. At face value, a high success ratio of asks to gifts could seem like a sign of success, but in her eyes there needs to be proper balance of failure to ensure the correct level of efficiency is achieved for the best possible results.

Success is a major theme of this book. It is filled with strategies that will enable you to enjoy more success and experience less failure. This does not mean that failure is always bad or something to be avoided at all costs. We could even argue that there is no such thing as failure, and that if you wait long enough and follow the causal chain of all failure, it will eventually lead to success. While this line of reasoning may be good for us in our personal lives, and may help to alleviate the fear of risk taking, it doesn't always work so well in an office setting.

In the professional setting, if failure is not followed by a breakthrough of some kind, be it growth or the success of an alternate attempt, it can have dire consequences. It is these consequences that we fear when faced with potential failure at work; this causes us to downplay our failures. It may also cause us to avoid risk-taking and to play it safe, so as to avoid any potentially negative impact from perceived failure. Not every failure is going to have an obvious connection to a positive impact. Because of this, we must try to create an environment where failure is acceptable because often the most successful projects are birthed out of a previous failure.

As a manager, you must allow and encourage your employees to take risks. Risk taking in a professional setting can lead to some amazing outcomes. However, when you take risks, there is a higher likelihood that you may fail. This is ok, but you have to monitor for real failure, as opposed to inevitable failure that is closely linked to breakthroughs and growth. A good manager will encourage a healthy amount of failure, and will not punish their employees for going out on a limb. The important thing, though, is to balance healthy failure versus repeated failure that is due to incompetence or negligence. Often when folks think of failure, they neglect to differentiate between the two.

Failure that is caused by a lack of knowledge that you should have is not good. Failure that is caused by negligence is not good. Failure that is caused by the expression of negative attributes, like lying or stealing someone else's work or ideas, is not good. These kinds of failure should not be tolerated, and we need to work to eradicate as much of this kind of failure as possible.

Failure that results from strategic risk taking is ok and is a necessary part of growth. Make sure you are taking risks and experimenting. Experimentation is fun. Take a step back from yourself and your work and operate like a scientist conducting an experiment. Find out what happens if you push this button or that button, if you say this to that person or show up to work in this or that way. Not all of your experiments will be ones that will make it into your toolbox to be repeated but you will never be able to forge new tools to enhance your output if you are not given the freedom to experiment or operate from a place of fear.

Remember that change is the essence of life. The state of failure will come and go. Allow it to run its course. Don't allow it to linger for too long and be ready to move on from it and put it behind you at the optimal speed. Sit with it and glean whatever fruit you are able to glean and then discard and move on. Not giving it more attention than it deserves. Knowing that it will pass should alleviate some of the fear that is caused by its potential presence.

Chapter 64

POLISHING YOU INTO A GEMSTONE

"Standing on a hill in the mountain of dreams,
telling myself it's not as hard, hard, hard as it seems"

Led Zeppelin,
Going to California

As this book draws to a close, I don't want to leave without saying a few words about haters. As we go through life, there will likely come a time where we have encounters with haters or negative influences that seek to cause you harm in some form or another. A hater is someone who most likely doesn't have your best interest at heart. They may try to hurt you in some way through sabotaging your work, your reputation, or your character. It is important to pay as little attention to haters as possible and give them as little validation, focus and energy as possible.

A little-known truth is that, when a hater is engaging in negative activity meant to bring you down, their negative energy is actually setting you on the course to success. This means that when a hater sets in motion something that they think is going to harm you, they have actually set in motion something that is going to strengthen you. For it is their negative act that gives birth to the conditions that eventually bring forth a positive in your life that might not have happened had the hater not tried to interfere. Meaning that it's the very act of trying to stop you from greatness that acts as a catalyst, and sparks the existence of your greatness into actuality. Think about this, look for examples of this in your own life, and I guarantee you'll find them.

The best example I can give is that of Gandhi and his life. If Gandhi were never thrown off of that first-class train in South Africa, he never would have embarked on the journey of fighting for--and winning-- equality for Indians in South Africa, and eventually freeing India from British occupation without firing a single bullet. Think about that for a minute. Gandhi's work resulted in India gaining its independence from one of the largest nation-states of the time. That one act from a hater, who tried to dim Gandhi's light, ended up setting the course for Gandhi's light to shine as bright as possible and sparked a chain reaction that allowed for so many other lights to shine.

A hater will try to make you believe that they are grinding you down into dust, but this is not possible. Don't fear the grind. ***You are a gemstone and cannot be ground into dust.*** A hater can never wield such power over you. They will try very hard to make you think they can. But in fact, a hater has zero power or influence over you. While, in their mind, as they introduce negativity after negativity, they think they are grinding you down into dust; in actuality, they are polishing your gemstone, so that you can shine bright like the gemstone you are.

Never fear a hater. They will try to convince you that they have power. Do not allow your mind to believe this. Know they have no power. Pay them no mind. Do not focus on them. Treat them as if they do not exist when they are not around. They are an apparition. If they are in your life in such a way that you have to interact with them, stay positive and polite. Keep your interactions to a minimum while simultaneously working on removing them completely from your regular interactions. Use your energy and focus to create a barrier between you and them.

If you do fear a hater, and anything negative comes about through your interactions, it is most likely due to your own fear and/or belief that they have power that is causing the disruption in your life, not them. Think of a hater like an apparition. It may seem scary, but it can't touch you. It can't affect you negatively in the way that they are trying to scare you into thinking they can. And again, anything they do set in motion will always bring about a huge positivity in your life that would have otherwise never been born.

What I also want you to know is that this is especially the case with your managers or colleagues when they are giving tough, constructive feedback. While this can feel negative, destructive, and painful; this is only because they are destroying old ways of being that are no longer serving you. They are forging you into a tool, polishing you so you can shine as bright as ever, so that you can activate more of your potential.

When you work in alignment with truth and disrupt the status quo for the betterment of your organization, you will sometimes find yourself in sticky situations. The system of this book is meant to help alleviate some of that, and to help give you the tools to navigate bad behaviors that may come your way. The world is the way it is because not everyone is working together for the betterment of each other; in your office, that translates to not being full service-oriented people.

Unfortunately, our current popular culture is set up to strengthen the muscle of being a hater. I really love to watch tv and movies and have spent way too much of my life doing so. I learned a lot about the world through growing up watching tv. I'm disappointed with the current offerings of entertainment today. I see this sway into shows and themes that are all geared around critiquing others and creating drama fueled fights by pitting friends against each other, inciting a fight and basking in the aftermath of the drama.

In fact, the very definition of 'drama' is shifting from an art that expresses and explores universal themes of the human condition in search for truth into some strange form of a gladiatorialized show of senseless negativity for the sake of generating artificial discord. This consistent display of people fighting each other and engaging in hater-offs is making it more difficult for us to be able to get along in our personal and professional lives and is creating more haters than have ever existed. This is why it is of prime importance to understand that haters are powerless apparitions that should be ignored and not engaged. ***When we engage with haters, we give them life with our energy; when we ignore them, they fade away.***

Maya Angelou said that, "When someone shows you who they are, believe them the first time." This will help you to avoid repeated disappointment and pain. Remember, anyone who is not aligned with truth has no power; their power is illusory. Don't fear apparitions. Move forward with the strategies in this book, and be courageous. Have no fear, things are not as hard as they may seem.

Chapter 65

BE COURAGEOUS

"Good things come to those that wait up, but don't wait to jump in too long. Don't sleep; you gotta stay up. Don't, don't sleep; you gotta stay up."

Miguel, "Skywalker"

This book focuses on concepts that lean towards the flow, and in so doing it may give off the impression that this is about being nice or continuing status quo; but this couldn't be further from the truth. These are all strategies that actually seek to push boundaries, and move the needle in a positive direction in a way that will guarantee impact. ***Move forward, and be courageous like a lion in everything you do.*** When the time calls to push harder and take a stand, take a stand! This means making potentially tough decisions and reaching down for that grit that's deep within.

Implementing the strategies in this book will often take courage, like speaking the right words at the right time. Finding a flow is one of the most important things you can do so that you can size it up, analyze, look for areas of strength and weakness, and then determine the best course of action to work alongside the flow to take advantage of the energy.

As you push it into new terrain and expand your energy's reach and/or change its course, it can achieve maximum positive impact. To do this requires presence, integrity, honesty, truth, strength, and resolve; it requires that you be an observer and dial into the DNA of your culture through connecting to the *Who*, *What*, *When*, *Where*, *Why*, and *How* of your surroundings at every moment, to live in this space and operate out of it. To do this, my friend, takes massive amounts of courage and steadfastness. As an influencer and change maker, you will disrupt. Disruption can result in curious behavior. Stay strong and continue to be courageous on behalf of the betterment of your collective organization. Ignore haters.

As a change-maker and disruptor, you will encounter situations of resistance. Be bold in the face of resistance to positive change and hold your ground. There is a quote by William Penn on the wall in the hallway near my office that says, "Right is right, even if everyone is against it, and wrong is wrong, even if everyone is for it." There have been numerous occasions where I have walked by that sign to garner strength in the face of difficult situations birthed from negative reactions to positive change. I am thankful for whoever put that there.

It is unfortunate for the change-maker, but nevertheless a part of the path of anyone who is attempting to drive improvements, to encounter negative reactions. Sometimes it's the most positive people who can have the most negative critics. Don't be discouraged if you are met with such criticism as it is usually a sign that you are on the right path and doing something meaningful and important. This book is an attempt to provide the change-maker with tools that can drastically reduce negative reactions to positive change so that the changes you put into motion are met with grace and are allowed to take root, flourish, flower and produce fruit.

Chapter 66

UNLIMITED POTENTIAL

We exist as pure potential.

We ourselves are the activation of infinity into being. We are a mix of the infinite blended with the temporal realm. We each have a unique set of limitations due to our unique physical composition, *but* ***we all have an equal share of the infinite***. We are limited by our temporal bodies, but have full access to the unlimited that we can tap into at any moment because we are made from it and of it and we live in it and we are forever connected to it. Through tapping into that infinite potential, ***we can bring essentially anything we want into existence. The process of creating something out of our potentiality and bringing it from the realm of the potential into the realm of the actual, is called activation.*** This is what we mean by activating. In order to thrive in this world, you must master this art of activation.

We are all amazing - and we are all capable of so much. Make sure you believe that, and don't get fooled into thinking you have limitations - sometimes it just takes some practice, and work, to perfect the art of activation; don't give up because you don't get it right on the first try - remember that you are this unique blend of infinite and finite – you can tap into your unlimited side without limit - and keep activating until you get better and better at the art of activation. Your unique blend of infinite and finite is what allows you to activate unique things into this world. ***Your limitations form the unique vantage point from which you always stand and observe, and through which you activate.***

You can go deep and explore this in the world, and it's amazing, but just be careful not to go too deep into the unlimited side. It's like structured versus unstructured data. The physical world is like structured data; when you dive into your unlimited side, you're getting into the source code of existence, and it's like you're dipping into unstructured data territory. As things start to lose structure, it becomes harder to understand how to reconcile the meaning of that with our structured half. Sometimes it's this inability to reconcile this structure/unstructure, and to provide some sort of mental structural rendering or meaning, that can cause issues within our minds resulting in confusion.

Because we come from the world of the unknown, the infinite, everything we give birth to also has this blend of the infinite and temporal, and can also have the power to activate. This means that our activations can potentially activate, and their activations can potentially activate and so on, *ad infinitum*. ***Our reach is limitless.*** This is an amazing thing. Think of all of the positive implications this has. Our reach is so far and deep. We are capable of moving so much with even the simplest of activations. With great power comes great responsibility, though. Take precautions to activate only things that are appropriate so as not to introduce highly destructive ricochets that cause unjust harm to life and existence.

Let's collectively use our power of activation to give rise to a movement to elevate our profession and create VPs and AVPs of Prospect Development or Advancement Services or whatever your prospect research/data management program is called so that our voices are heard and our influence can lead to more dollars in the door, the creation of the ultimate donor experienced and the fulfillment of the missions of our organizations. Together we will get there.

Let's not allow negativity and pessimism to take hold of our associations and instead create an environment of welcoming and positivity and teamwork and inclusion for all.

Let's create an environment amongst our peers in the Prospect Development data community that is one of unity and collaboration and cooperation. One that seeks to build each other up. One that celebrates each other's successes.

Let's set up positive partnerships, with mutual respect, built on equal footing, with our constituents/fundraisers across all departments in development.

Let's create environments of inclusiveness and freedom so that our creative genius can realize full activation.

We have the power to change our fates and the fates of those that come behind us through thinking big, implementing *Precision Prospect Development* strategies and never giving up.

The only way for our organizations to continue to thrive in the future is to invite us into a seat of influence. Go and RSVP your spot now.

As we push further along on this journey, and make it over all of our obstacles and hurdles and usher in a new era in our field, the words of ***the little engine that could*** resonate and reverberate:

I thought I could.

I thought I could.

I thought I could.

In the words of the song Magic, as sung by Olivia Newton John:

You have to believe we are magic
nothing can stand in our way
you have to believe we are magic
don't let your aim ever stray
and if all your hopes survive
Destiny will arrive
and bring all your dreams alive
for you

ABOUT THE AUTHOR

Nathan Fay is a leading figure in the nonprofit industry and currently serves as Associate Vice President of Prospect Development at City of Hope, one of the nation's top National Cancer Institutes. Previously, he spent over 11 years in various roles at Stanford University, including 7 years as Director of Data Analytics and Prospect Research for the Children's Hospital.

In addition, Nathan is a sought-after speaker in management philosophy, business intelligence and artificial intelligence. He is a scholar of philosophical systems with an emphasis on applying philosophy and technology to create a more socially just society.

He coined the term "Precision Philanthropy" to refer to a future-state, cybernetic structure, that utilizes artificial intelligence technologies to dramatically enhance efficiency in the nonprofit sector. Nathan is the author of Precision Prospect Development.

Nathan currently serves on the Artificial Intelligence in Advancement Advisory Council. He previously served on the board of CARA (California Advancement Researchers Association).

www.ingramcontent.com/pod-product-compliance
Lightning Source LLC
Chambersburg PA
CBHW021529210326
41599CB00012B/1436